THE ADULT AND THE NURSERY SCHOOL CHILD

The Adult and the Nursery School Child

Second edition

MARGARET I. FLETCHER

Supervisor of the Nursery School Division (retired 1965)
and Assistant Professor of Child Study
Institute of Child Study
University of Toronto

with Foreword by
W.E. BLATZ, M.A., M.B., Ph.D.
Director, Institute of Child Study 1925-1960

Illustrated by
Marjorie Wilson

University of Toronto Press

ISBN 0-8020-2167-0
LC 59-4886

This book was written and
prepared in part with the aid of
Canadian Federal Health Grant 605-5-147

Foreword

This foreword is about the author, not about the book. It will speak for itself!

Of course, the reader may very readily read between the lines and interpret quite accurately the personality of the author. A reader is always impelled to try to discern the personality behind the production, at the time or in retrospect. The number of biographies of literary figures upholds this tenet. These short paragraphs may help to make this task easier. After all, an author is always more fascinating than the book he or she writes.

"Fletch," as she was very early in her career called by her young charges, violated several myths. In the first place, she is a spinster, traditionally a person not supposed to know much about young children. The skill which she very early acquired in handling them could certainly not be ascribed to "mother-instinct." As her mentor, whom she very early surpassed, I was fascinated by her growing ingenuity and *savoir faire*. On one occasion when she was assisting in the care of the Dionne quintuplets,* she was conversing with Mrs. Dionne, whose English was as inadequate as Fletch's French. "Combien d'enfants avez-vous?" asked Mrs. Dionne. Fletch, catching the word "enfants," thought she was asking about the enrolment in the Nursery School of which she was principal, and answered, "Trent-et-deux," to which the wholly understandable respect of the interlocutor could only be expressed by "Mon Dieu!"

* The Dionne quintuplets were born in Callander, Ontario, May 28th, 1934. This was a spectacular event which received much publicity from the press and radio. Thousands of visitors from all over the world came to see them. Dr. Blatz and his staff both supervised their living arrangements programme and studied the development of these identical siblings in their early years. All sisters lived to adulthood and three are still living.

Fletch never permits the theories we propound to interfere with what she knows is right for the welfare of the children. However, she has her own system. A critic would quite readily ascribe this system partly to the pragmatism of William James, and partly to the inventiveness and aliveness of the much maligned John Dewey. This would be a keen commentary on her methodology, except for the fact that it was almost fully developed by her before she ever read either one of these philosophers.

Exploding a second myth, after nearly three decades of teaching, singing, composing songs and plays, and lecturing, she has turned the clock back. She certainly *has* more energy than she has ever had. Only her assistants are tired at the end of the day!

Thirdly, she has accomplished, to a large degree, the difficult task of reconciling a benevolent authoritarianism ("discipline *is* important") with a discriminating permissiveness ("if you interfere too much, take a rest!"). Another paradox is that through it all shines an emotional calmness that is the epitome of sentiment without being sentimental.

To paraphrase a saying which has dubiously been ascribed to St. Augustine, it can truly be said of Fletch, "Give me a child between two and five, and I will work wonders." She, of course, would *not* say so herself.

Read and judge.

W.E. BLATZ

Geryfield Farm
Caledon East
April 1958

Acknowledgements

I wish to express my indebtedness to the many members of staff who worked with me in the nursery school of the Institute of Child Study and helped to evolve the plan for guiding preschool children presented in this book.

M.I.F.

Contents

Introduction to the second edition

Margaret Fletcher wrote this book in the mid fifties. It grew out of her thirty years experience as supervisor of the St. George's Nursery School at the Institute of Child Study, University of Toronto, and is based on the material she gave in the first part of her annual series of lectures to students in nursery education. It describes ways by which daily living can be effectively planned in the nursery school so that good human relations between adults and children can be developed. It was thought, and still is, that good human relationships form the essential groundwork from which growth in skills and personality is made possible. Without this groundwork either nothing develops, or else a pseudo-growth which is always precarious.

In re-reading the book fifteen years later, there is very little that needs changing. The preschool field has greatly expanded[1] but daily living in the nursery schools and day care centres is composed of the same elements, adults and children and the relationships and interaction between them. The practices Professor Fletcher describes are still an effective means of making nursery living salutary for all involved in it.

These procedures drawn from her experience of working with "normal" children in a laboratory school, will of course be only guidelines for practices in other types of centres. For example, the requirements here suggested will be greatly modified in centres for all day care as well as in specialized units for retarded, disturbed, deprived or handicapped children, but there still will be require-

1 For example in the province of Ontario in 1958 there were 291 licensed preschool units, a staff of about 450 serving 10,650 children. In November 1973, there were 940 units, a staff of 4,000 for 36,950 children.

ments; the "personal contacts" will be adapted to meet the needs of children coming from homes where little is given; the suggestions for handling clothing and nourishment will be adjusted to the type of community and climatic conditions of the nursery; and indeed, much of what is said herein will be varied by the philosophy of the group who have established and are in charge of the centre.

Dr. W.E. Blatz was director of the Institute of Child Study of which the nursery school Miss Fletcher supervised was one important part. It is not surprising therefore that the plan she here describes reflects a very clear and definite system of developmental psychology, namely the Blatz theory of human security. This he has fully stated in his book *Human Security: Some Reflections*.[2] Blatz views development as change from *immature dependency* (complete reliance on others), towards a balance between *mature dependence* (a give and take with others), and *independence* (a willingness to rely on oneself). The secure person is he who can make his own decisions and is willing to accept the consequences of them. Blatz believed the nursery years were extremely important in fostering the development of security, therefore nursery life had to provide experience for the children in both making decisions and accepting consequences of them at their own level of maturity, and also in discovering the rudiments of interaction on an equal basis with their peers. It is believed that attainment of human security would result both in individual mental health and community social health.

Virtues of Miss Fletcher's book are its straightforwardness and simplicity. In these days when the cultural pattern demands books that are bigger and bigger (and perhaps say less and less) and where obscurity is often accepted as implying profundity (though it may be only gobbledygook) it is refreshing to be told practically and simply, ways by which daily living in a nursery school can be satisfying and effective. We should be grateful to Miss Fletcher for condensing experience of a lifetime into a short book and for making each sentence say what she means.

Much of course is not included. The book does not purport to describe development through the preschool years; it does not touch

2 An abbreviated version is given in *Readings in Child Development* by Brockman, Whiteley and Zubek. (Toronto 1973)

on pathology of child growth; it does not discourse on cognitive skills of the preschool child nor educational methods of preparing him for his academic life. These can be found in other books, some of which are given in the bibliography, and reference is made to them in the Epilogue. It confines itself to one thing—a plan by which daily life in the nursery can be enjoyable and effective and adults and children find their rightful roles.

This new edition is greatly enhanced by the Epilogue that Professor Dorothy Millichamp has written for it. Her review of trends in Child Study from the twenties to the present is no dry treatise. She describes a sequence which she has lived through from her student days with the textbook by Harriet Johnson to her recent involvement with research on the intellect of young children based on the Guilford model.

Professor Millichamp was assistant director to Dr. Blatz from 1932 until 1960. Her main activity was running "upstairs and down" between the academic staff and the nursery school. As she discussed new discoveries with students upstairs, she was aware of (indeed involved in) the effect these were having on the playground and playrooms below. She writes of a period of child study in which she continually participated and which, in no small way, influenced in Canada.

MARY L. NORTHWAY
The Brora Centre, Toronto, Canada
1974

THE ADULT AND THE NURSERY SCHOOL CHILD

1.   What should our plan be?

All adults have a very great obligation to children; an obligation to help them grow. Some people look upon bringing up children as a colossal undertaking, too complicated to face. They become intense and uncertain and take their responsibility far too seriously. They forget that helping children grow is a natural function to be enjoyed by both child and adult alike. However, other people do not take this responsibility quite seriously enough. They forget that, from the day a child is born, it is the adults in his life who are responsible for his growth and well-being and who can help him develop as a person in his own right.

Adults are often confused by all the theories they hear of what is the best thing to do for a young child. They hear of the value of permitting a child to do pretty much as he likes and, at the same time, are aware of the theory that children should be required by adults to move and act in a definite pattern. They hear that children should be placed in a group of other children and allowed to learn by experience, bitter or otherwise. They hear that all that is necessary for a young child is love and care from adults. All of these theories have some truth in them, which makes it confusing if an adult tries to decide which is right and which is wrong. Obviously,

3

what is needed is a plan that takes into account all the important values.

This book is concerned with the time of a child's life when he is growing from two to five years of age, and we hope that the way of guiding this age group in nursery school, which is unfolded here, will be a help to all adults working with such children whether a child remains at home during these years or whether he goes to a nursery school.

If a child goes to a nursery school, the teachers in it share with his parents the obligation that adults have towards children. Nursery school teachers, accepting this responsibility towards children, must first know what takes place in the world of most pre-school children. So, let us take a look at a young child's day and then consider what he *could* be learning in it.

A pre-school child's day is divided, more or less, into routines and playtime. Generally speaking, his routines are those of dressing and undressing, washing, toilet, sleeping and eating. In them, he has an opportunity to achieve some physical skill according to his ability. He can be learning not only that these are details of his personal life that must be done, but also that they are worth his interest and effort. He can be learning, slowly, to take responsibility for these details himself, while accepting willingly and happily the direction and help of adults.

A pre-school child's playtimes usually include outdoor active play, indoor quieter play, group and individual play, times of music, dancing, story, and special activities. In his play, he could be acquiring purposeful play habits and learning to depend on himself for ideas. As his interests and skills increase, he could be learning to express these ideas constructively and creatively.

Because adults know that a young child should be experiencing the enjoyment of companionship, his life will be arranged to include a time when he can be with other children more or less of the same age. One of the first things a child learns is that all other children are also human beings and different in many ways from each other and from himself. Gradually, he can become aware not only that *he* has his rights but also that each other child, as a separate individual, has rights equal to his own. Slowly he can learn to appreciate and consider the rights of the other children. At first, younger children will play happily side by side, each with his own interest and paying little attention to each other. Soon, however, they start to play together in small groups of three and four, stimulated by each other's ideas and learning to play co-operatively with one another. Playing together, they have an opportunity to learn the give and take necessary in all our lives. Slowly they can be helped to discover that consideration of one another is worthwhile because it means that there will be a mutual acceptance of each other and enjoyment in being together.

However, not all a child's social experiences are with children and a great deal of a child's day is spent with adults. The relationship between a child and adults is an essential part of his growing up. He can be learning that depending on the adults around him and accepting their guidance is natural and right and, equally, he can be learning that these adults will support him in his growing independence. He can be learning that the adults he knows have rights, even as he has, and that these must be considered, but he can also be discovering the wonderful experience of adult and child working and playing and living with one another and the happiness of sharing new experiences together. Through this kind of relationship, the child will be learning to trust and respect his adults.

As he slowly grows, a child can be developing attitudes of enthusiasm and *joie de vivre* and the qualities of consideration, gentleness and understanding of others. One of the ways he acquires these qualities is from the attitudes of the adults with whom he lives.

In all his daily experiences, a child can be learning to feel free to express his enjoyment and enthusiasms and, at the same time, to accept experiences of anger and fear and how to deal with these. A young child has little or no control over his emotions. When he feels angry, he will act angrily and when he is afraid, he will act fearfully. Gradually, he can learn to control his expression of anger and he can be helped to replace his fears with an eagerness to explore and experiment with his world around him.

All this, then, is what a pre-school child could be learning. But it is only through the adults in his world and through the plan which they make for him, that this learning can be achieved. How vital it is, then, that there should be a plan which considers the importance of *all* these aspects of a child's development: a plan which provides opportunities for the child to take responsibility and to grow in and enjoy independence; opportunities for him to have social experiences; opportunities for emotional expression and also for learning emotional control; opportunities for him to learn in his routines and play. Above all, there should be a plan which considers the importance of the relationship between a child and his adults.

The content of this book is based on such a plan and reflects the belief that a child learns from the adults with whom he lives and through the plan which they have devised to help him grow.

2. Teacher and child

The most important things about a nursery school are stated in the title of this chapter, "Teacher and Child." Teachers and children are the human beings who live and move, grow and learn, within the nursery school walls. So, in this chapter, we shall discuss first, teachers, then children and then, finally, the most important word in our chapter title, AND, for this implies the relationship that exists between teachers and children, children and teachers.

I. THE TEACHER

Most of us can imagine an ideal nursery school teacher just as we can imagine the saints, although we have never seen one and never expect to. No actual teacher reaches the ideal, but this should not concern us too much because it is the variations among nursery school teachers that make life rich and interesting. It is because some nursery school teachers have qualities that others lack and still others have qualities that are rare in the rest of a group, that, in a team, they can accomplish what they want to achieve. Ideals, after all, are something to be attempted, though they may not always be attained. So, as we discuss qualities of the ideal, we should remember that all nursery school teachers possess these to some extent, but each in different proportions. A person who is completely lacking in any of these qualities should probably not go into nursery school work. A person who has all of them blended in perfect proportion would be a treasure that is rarely found in the practical world of nursery living.

Naturalness. Years of working with and training nursery school teachers have suggested that the quality of being natural is all-important.

The person who feels natural with children and with her colleagues and who is at ease in being herself has a great advantage. The extent to which she can do so depends, of course, upon how much the rest of the staff accepts her as she is and for what she is. It will also increase as she becomes more familiar with the ways of the nursery school world. There are few teachers who, on their first day, or even in their first month in a nursery school, feel completely at ease. If they do, it is perhaps a fault, a lack of awareness of how much they have to learn.

It would not be desirable for a teacher to become the mere image of someone she considers to be a highly successful figure in nursery school work. She should not attempt to act exactly as Miss K. does simply because Miss K. has techniques that she uses with success. Nor should a teacher attempt to be a paragon of all the virtues. Rather, she should try to assimilate wise ways of nursery school procedures and make them her own.

Knowledge. A good nursery school teacher has real knowledge of children. And there is a tremendous amount of knowledge about children in the 1970's. Library shelves are filled with volumes on how children develop and a nursery school teacher will be imbued with the wisdom that has been garnered by thoughtful scientists and clinicians. However, knowledge in itself is not enough. In fact, taken in too large doses and not balanced with understanding of practical experience, it may indeed become harmful. Scientists do not make the best nursery school teachers. Their hard-won trait of objectivity, which is so important in enabling them to make new discoveries about children, can be a definite handicap when they are involved in caring for them. In the same way, much as the wealth of clinical materials has contributed to our understanding of children, some clinicians may find it difficult to work in a nursery school, particularly if the school is designed for well and normal children. A good nursery school teacher certainly needs to know all that she can about children. However, she must be cautious lest she be carried away by each new idea that she encounters in a book, and hesitant about adapting her procedures on the spur of the moment to someone's new theories. She should keep an open mind, ready to consider new ideas and, gradually, to incorporate into her thinking that which has been proved true.

✓*Judgement*. Balancing this knowledge, then, the teacher must have a *feel* for children. What this means is hard to define. It might be called good judgement or an ability to make wise decisions or, perhaps, just common sense. We mean that she should be a person who is aware of what is going on about her and what needs to be done about it, not in terms of theory, but in terms of the particular situation and of the needs and capabilities of the children with whom she works. For example, one cold day in the playground Bobby takes off his mitts. The teacher tells him to put them on again. Bobby says, "But Miss Brown, my hands are warm." The teacher feels his hands; they *are* warm; and she sensibly adds, "Of course, you don't need your mitts." Another example might be the following incident. Mary was a new little girl who did not like to play with any of the outdoor equipment, although indoors she would play happily with plasticene. As a general rule, plasticene is kept for indoors only, but the teacher took plasticene out to the playground for Mary. She played contentedly with it for days. Soon she became interested in the sand box and the kiddy kars and the plasticene could be left indoors. Another example of good common sense is provided by the handling of a child refusing to drink up the fruit juice he usually enjoyed; the teacher would immediately realize that this was unusual and that perhaps the child was sick, and would let him leave it for that day.

✓*Assurance*. A quality that has appeared to be very important in a nursery school teacher is that of assurance. This does not mean the pseudo-assurance of people who command children in the manner of sergeant-majors. Rather, it is that quiet inner quality that comes from a basic feeling of confidence in oneself and what one is doing. It conveys to a child that his teacher knows what she is doing, and the child feels protected by this assurance and is willing to accept her decisions. If a teacher is uncertain and filled with doubts, children will catch these doubts and become uncertain too. Assurance is conveyed not only in what is done. To a great extent, it is also conveyed by the voice—what is said and how it is said.

Self-control. Of course, every teacher should have developed a good deal of self-control. In adults, self-control does not mean merely controlling anger and fear. One rarely encounters a teacher who loses her temper and stamps her feet, or one who allows her fear to drive her from her duties. The self-control that is important is far more sophisticated than this. It means that a teacher is able to put her work before her personal feelings. At times, children will be trying to any nursery school teacher. If she has self-control, she will not do what would most quickly relieve her irritation, but rather act according to what is best for the children, knowing full well that an exasperating child probably needs as much, if not more, help than anyone else in her group.

Then, too, there may be many difficulties in the personal life of a teacher. It is hard to do a good job when one is worried about one's own problems. It is very difficult indeed to have some thrilling personal news and not discuss it with associates while supervising the playground. By self-control, then, is meant more than keeping one's temper. We mean that the children must come first, despite a teacher's own personal feelings and emotions.

Of course, a teacher's personal life has a place too in the nursery school and children will be delighted to see their teacher's new coat or, perhaps, to celebrate her birthday. Again, most nursery schools will see that times are provided when the staff and students are free to talk among themselves about anything they like. But the tea hour or the coffee hour is the time for this sort of thing; in the playroom, it becomes only a discord.

Feelings. The last thing in the world to be desired is that teachers should appear to be spiritless creatures without any emotion within them. Children must not learn to think of adults as creatures who are never afraid, never angry, never excited, never thrilled, never interested. The point, really, is to express those feelings which are appropriate to the situation. For instance, if a child begins to cry when he hears a loud clap of thunder, a teacher will give him more assurance by saying, "I don't like it much either," than by pretending that she has no feelings at all about it. Children can see very quickly through façades. As a teacher, she must learn to control the expression of feelings so that what she says and does has some relevance to the child's world.

Seriousness. It goes without saying that a nursery school teacher should be serious. That is, she should take her work, as she would in any profession, seriously. We do not mean to imply here that a teacher should be serious about every little detail of the nursery school day and go around with furrowed brow, worrying lest the paint brushes go into the wrong box. Nor should she be in a state of continual anxiety about things that may never happen. A school in which the staff members look like solemn owls might be interesting to the ornithologist, but certainly not to anyone else. However, a teacher *will* have to take seriously her responsibility for the many details which are important in a child's day.

Humour. The ability to see the humour in situations keeps a teacher from becoming over-serious and intense about her responsibilities. A sense of humour is really a sense of proportion, the ability to see things in a proper perspective. But forced humour only creates an artificial situation. The value of humour depends upon appropriateness. We must learn to choose what we laugh at and with whom we laugh. Adult humour is different from child humour. Adults often forget this and laugh at something a child has said in all seriousness. The child then becomes self-conscious and uncomfortable in his embarrassment. Needless to say, to ridicule a child or to be sarcastic with him is not amusing. Nor should an adult's comments ever seem to make fun of children.

Naturally, many times throughout the day, teacher and child will laugh together at what the child is enjoying and, of course, after school is over, teachers will often laugh among themselves at the many wonderfully funny things the children say. Children are fun and adults can be fun too. It is a pity when a teacher is too busy and too serious to realize that there are plenty of opportunities in a nursery school where teacher and child can find this out together.

This need not lead to a teacher's behaving in a silly or affected way. To do so would make her look ridiculous and often embarrasses the children.

Easiness. Another quality of our ideal nursery school teacher is that she should be relaxed and appear leisurely. Such a characteristic comes fundamentally from her own feeling of security and ease of mind. However, an impression of being relaxed and at ease can be given through deliberate attempt and careful planning. Some nursery school teachers dart about as if they were in a school of fish rather than children. Each thing that occurs strikes their eyes and they dash to do this and the other thing, as if each incident signalled a major catastrophe. Where then is the easy and relaxed atmosphere we seek for the nursery school?

Alertness. Certainly, a teacher will be aware of her responsibility towards other people's children. She will know that hazardous situations can occur and will be constantly alert to what is going on about her. She should be able to anticipate situations and, by a word here or a word there, avert them before they develop. When emergencies do occur, a teacher must be ready to meet them. Contingencies will be met by planning, not by dashing. A teacher will learn what to do in fire or flood; when a child is taken ill; or when half the staff is absent. Plans will have been made to meet such situations. Most emergencies occur only when there is lack of planning and lack of foresight as to how possible situations will be dealt with. The willingness of a teacher to understand and to adhere to such plans is one of her most valuable qualities.

Some nursery school teachers develop a tendency to classify anything out of the ordinary as an emergency. This comes from a failure of their sense of perspective. They see little things as too big and get into a turmoil about it. Such teachers would be wise to recall the words of a well-known doctor, "There are only three emergencies—haemorrhage, childbirth and poisoning. In any other circumstances, walk, don't run; and remember that your plans, not your perspiration, will carry you through."

We would hope, then, that our nursery school teacher would possess the qualities that have been described. She would know and be herself. She would have knowledge of and a feeling for children. She would be aware of her responsibilities. She would be serious but not solemn or worried. She would be wise in making decisions. She would have assurance and self-control. Her humour would be fun, but kindly fun. She would appear to have that peace of mind that enables her to be relaxed and leisurely and, at the same time, competent to meet all situations of the nursery school world.

II. THE CHILD

Most young teachers who go into nursery school work know something about children. Few of them, however, know very much about pre-school children, for they are not likely to have younger brothers and sisters of this age group, and they are usually too young to have children, of their own. Unless a young teacher has taught Sunday School or done baby-sitting, her contacts with this age group will be few and she may be quite bewildered by young children.

This book cannot begin to tell all that is known about children of this age. There has probably been more study done of this age than of any other. A teacher will gain this knowledge through books and courses on child development but, finally, through her actual work with children, she will gain her real understanding of them.

Immaturity. There are, however, three things of particular importance of which a new teacher should be made aware and which she should never forget. The first is the essential immaturity of the nursery school child. At this age, a child does not behave according to adult standards and he will need great understanding as he learns. He is just in the process of learning the skills of daily living; so a teacher must not expect him to do very much for himself and he will need care, protection and help. His emotional responses are unpredictable and he requires help with these. His skills of play, both with materials and with other children, are quite naïve, and therefore a teacher may have to help him learn how to play.

Learning. The second thing a teacher should realize is that, even though pre-school children are immature, they are the fastest learners in the world. Development during the nursery school years goes on so rapidly that the contrast between a two-year-old and a four-year-old is quite spectacular. After all, between two and four, a child has doubled his age. To some adults, the achievement of a nursery school child may appear trivial but the teacher who compares the skills of these two ages knows that an amazing amount has happened in the two years. Therefore, although a teacher should be very much aware of the essential immaturity of the child, she will realize that he can learn very quickly and that, step by step, a surprising amount of progress can be expected.

Differences. The third thing a teacher should know before she begins to work with children, is the vast difference that exists among them, even at this early age. No matter what rules or general procedures are followed, these are adaptable and adapted, modified and transformed, to meet the particular capabilities and personalities of each child. The over-all principles remain but the ways in which they are effected differ. For example, in the general procedure of a nursery school dining-room, a child is expected to eat his dinner before his dessert; but a child who may have less appetite than the others would be served a much smaller helping. Or, for another example, while most children join in the music and story times with enthusiasm, one might, at first, feel shy about it and be reluctant to come with the others. A teacher can arrange, for *him*, a story time with perhaps only one other child to begin with, or have him "just watch" the others, perhaps sitting on the teacher's lap. A very shy child might take several weeks before he feels easy and comfortable and ready to join the other children. A teacher realizes that children are different from one another. She accepts each child for what he is and adapts her procedures to meet these differences.

III. THE TEACHER AND THE CHILD

When a child comes to nursery school, he begins to form his first relationships with adults outside his own home. These contacts are extremely important because what he learns to expect from his teachers will influence his attitudes towards adults in general and towards the wide world which he now starts to encounter. His teachers, naturally, will not try to take the place of his mother, but the child should find them warm, affectionate and deeply interested in him. This will mean that he will now have two groups of adults concerned about him: his parents at home and his teachers at school.

Affection. Nursery school teachers love children. They always have and they always will. But, for a long time we have tried to keep away from using the word "love" because it can lead to a confusion of meanings, one of these having an over-sentimental connotation. One might use the word "interest," meaning a deep and personal interest which would show in everything the teacher said or did. But, perhaps, after all, we *should* call it "love" because nursery school teachers *do* love children. Nothing is too much to ask and no effort is too great to make for the children. The bond between teacher and child, of course, is not love in exactly the same sense as is the bond between parent and child but, nevertheless, it is a love of children which is real, unchanging and very, very understanding.

Care. What this feeling is called does not matter as much as the manner in which it is expressed. Expression of it follows two channels, the first being the thoroughness, thoughtfulness and concern with which the adults plan the nursery school world and the nursery school life of the children. Making the environment a fit place for children to live in and providing a programme geared to the needs and interest of children takes infinite time and continual willingness to improve. Yet, it is through this kind of effort that a nursery school is created in which children can grow and which they will enjoy.

Expression. The second way by which the relationship is expressed is through the communication with each other of adult and child. The friendliness and affection of his teacher assures a child of the reality of this relationship. How unnatural and absurd to think that, with a young child, an adult should try to be impersonal or hide her feelings. A teacher need never feel embarrassed in showing the sentiment she feels. However, she must not demonstrate her affection to the point of bothering the child or interfering with him as he pursues his own interests. Nor should she use this sentiment to persuade a child to do what he must do. For example, for an adult to say to a child, "If you love me you will do thus and so," or "I won't love you any more if you do that," really amounts to using affection as a bribe. We want the child to know that our affection for him does not change, even though sometimes we have to disapprove of his behaviour.

A great deal of a teacher's feeling for a child is expressed as she talks to him; so she will talk to him with both warmth and respect. Gushing and baby talk are as unnatural as is the other extreme of talking like a detached and objective scientist. Teachers should speak naturally to children as one human being to another.

Endearments. Children like to be addressed by their own names: John (or Johnny), Deborah (or Debbie). This helps them to feel that they are important as individuals. But there is no need to eliminate terms of endearment altogether. An occasional "dear" or "my dear" adds to a child's awareness of an adult's affection for him. Using terms of endearment constantly, however, can easily become merely a habit of speech which has lost its meaning altogether. To call a child "darling" or "honey" is natural enough too, once in a while, but used often the terms are apt to sound rather affected and artificial.

Listening. Important as it is that we speak to children clearly, sensibly and with respect for their identity as persons, it is essential that we also listen to what they want to tell us and try to understand. Much of a young child's life is spent in trying to persuade busy people to listen to what he has to say. Frequently he is frustrated and, sometimes, this is unavoidable, as for instance, in the cloakroom where he would find it too difficult to think of what he is doing and relate some news at the same time. Nor can he expect a teacher's personal attention in the story time where other children are more interested in hearing the teacher's story than in listening to him. Usually, however, a teacher *can* listen to a child and she must learn to be a good listener. She must receive what a child wants to tell her with attention and intelligence. She must learn to wait if he falters in his words, to give him time to repeat if she cannot understand him and, above all, she must be interested in what he has to tell her, knowing that it is of interest to him.

Touch. Because young children are not very versed in language, much communication is made through touch. A teacher will carry in her arms a frightened, tired or hurt child. She will often take a child on her lap and give many a little hug. She will always take his hand when he offers it to her. No contact a child makes should ever be rejected. While we don't ask him to accept ours, we should always accept his. However, such contacts will not be prolonged, for very soon children discover that there are far more interesting things to do in nursery school than to hold hands with adults. It should be remembered, too, that when a child goes home, he will have many opportunities for cuddling; for being bounced in the air by an affectionate father and soothed to sleep by a loving mother. Such contacts are rightly the privilege of the parents. Of course, when a child is in a living-in institution, the relationship between teacher and child will be a much closer one than in a part-time nursery school.

Group awareness. Something quite new happens to a child when he comes to nursery school. He has been used to relationships in which he himself and only two or three other people figure. For the first time in his life, he finds himself a member of a much larger group of individuals. This new experience may be something of a shock to him. For one thing, he is no longer so important and, for another, he must now share his adults with other children. All nursery school children will take time to adjust to this new situation and some will take longer than others. It is important to help a child be aware that a personal relationship between himself and his teacher exists and will continue, even though he is a member of a group.

Individual attention. This means there must be plenty of times in the day when a child is given the individual attention of his teacher. For instance, the routines can be planned so that the children come to the cloakroom or washroom one or two at a time. In this way, each child can have the teacher all to himself for a few moments. The teacher can show a personal interest in what the child is doing in his play by having a little conversation with him, encouraging him in his activities, approving his ideas and achievements, or working with him on a special project.

If a child becomes tired or bewildered in group situations, his teacher can arrange that he play by himself if he wants to or, perhaps, she can spend a little time with him looking at a book or just talking. Frequently, with a new child, she may have to entertain him, especially if that is the only kind of relationship he has been used to. Throughout his nursery school years, the teacher will be ready to help the child and to offer her ideas and suggestions as he needs and wants them. As teacher and child do things together, the relationship between them grows and the child realizes that, even as a member of a group, he will have her personal interest too.

Group attention. However, as a child grows older, he will inevitably become a member of a group. In the nursery school, there are many situations where children are dealt with together, such as story and music times, fire drill, coming in from the garden in the rain. These are valuable group experiences and a child should enjoy them. The way in which his teacher directs the group as a whole and her own interest and enthusiasm in these group experiences, will help the child to enjoy them.

Sometimes, a teacher becomes so interested in the group that she forgets about individuals. On the other hand, she may be so busy giving individual attention that she does not notice what is happening to the rest of the group. Nursery schools are no different from any other organization—schools, academic staffs, industrial groups, or the services—in having the baffling problem of the individual and the group. How much individual contact should there be? How much contact with the group? No one has answered these questions anywhere. The best that can be said is that, in a nursery school, a teacher must develop her own skill in giving attention to the group as well as to the individual. As she controls the group, each child in it should be able to trust her and depend on her, even as he does in his personal experiences.

Teachers and children, then, live together in a nursery school. The kind of relationship that is formed between them depends on what the teachers are and on what they do. This is an exceedingly important relationship because it can be one of the greatest influences in a child's life.

If a child is willing to try for himself, not fearing that he will make a mistake, not anxious as to whether he can "do it right," but enthusiastic in his own effort; if he is growing in independence and self-confidence while continuing to depend on and trust his teacher; and above all, if adult and child are enjoying one another; then, in the teacher-child relationship, all is indeed well.

3. Setting the stage

The plan by which a nursery school is organized grows out of what the staff wants to accomplish and the understanding that they may have of children. Nursery schools vary in their procedures and plans, partly because they differ in their understanding of children's development and partly because they establish different goals. All nursery schools, however, operate on some plan. In some, the plan is consciously and clearly stated; in others, it is implicit rather than verbally defined.

Self-effort. The foundations for any plan lie basically in the physical environment which is provided. Young children are and, of course, must be highly dependent on adults, but a child also needs to have an opportunity to enjoy doing things on his own and to gain self-confidence from it. It is at nursery school that the beginnings of self-effort and independence are discovered.

Of course, for both children and adults, physical environment determines, to a great extent, whether it is possible for them to do things by their own efforts or not. We often discover this in our own houses. If we have an old-fashioned dining-room table that must be

20

pulled from both ends whenever we want to add an extra leaf, we must, of necessity, depend upon someone else every time we want to enlarge or shorten our dining board. Old-fashioned houses, with their kitchens and pantries, required the help of three or four people to produce a meal. Modern kitchens, however, are so arranged that almost anyone can, through his own unaided effort, prepare the same meal.

It is the same with a nursery school. If it is designed so that it is possible for children to do things for themselves, they gain the experience and the pleasure of doing so. If, however, shelves are high and taps hard to turn, a child will have to ask an adult to help him each time he uses them. Indeed, because we have not always thought of physical environment as being so important, we have forced children into being continually dependent or else into attempting activities that are too difficult and, therefore, discouraging. So, nursery schools should review all the aspects of its physical set-up to see how much of a child's daily life can be carried out through his own effort. It is wise to consider the space and floor plan and the furnishings in terms of their making it possible for a child to function independently and, because we know that a child will put forth more effort if he is interested, we should make sure that there is provision for equipment that will prove interesting to him. It is through this effort that his skills begin and his constructive and creative play habits are formed.

Danger. Running into dangerous situations can impede a child's self-effort. If he hurts himself severely, or even slightly, he may not venture as confidently as before. Furthermore, it is the teacher's responsibility to protect him from danger. Therefore, in planning physical arrangements, anything that might be too hazardous for the children should be eliminated.

Companionship. One of the most important areas in which a child's independence grows is his life with other children. Therefore, we should be sure that he has an opportunity to enjoy companionship. For this, a nursery school provides a perfect situation. However, when young children are together many difficulties, indeed dangers, may arise. Children, themselves, have few skills, either of communication or for social control. Because of this, social situations, to a large extent, have to be planned for them. In arranging a physical set-up, the social readiness of the children is considered and the playground and playrooms, the cloakrooms, washrooms and dining-rooms designed with this in mind.

Order. Much of the activity of both children and adults depends on a fact that is so obvious we are usually unaware of it: that the world in which we live itself has a regularity and order. Night follows day, summer is followed by autumn. Sunday always comes between Saturday and Monday. The months of the year, the days of the week and the hours of the day run in orderly progress. The orderliness in our physical environment gives us a basis for confidence in what comes next and, therefore, in planning what we are going to do.

For a young child, such order is even more important and must exist in the events of his daily life. Therefore, in a nursery school, it is desirable to keep daily patterns fairly consistent. The children find what Blatz called a "dependent security"* in this consistency and, because they know what to expect, they are also able to initiate and carry out their own activity within this framework. This does not mean that each day is exactly the same as every other. The order underlying each day remains constant; the events which take place differ. That is, lunch always follows playtime and sleep always follows lunch; but lunch may be a typical lunchtime in the dining-room, or, on a beautiful spring day, it may be a picnic on the lawn.

The growth of children in self-effort then, depends on the physical setup in which they live. The equipment and plans of a nursery school should be considered in terms of whether or not they allow a child to function by himself; whether they will stimulate his interest; whether they protect him from danger; whether they provide for satisfying social experiences; and whether they convey a sense of order so that he knows what to expect from the world in which he lives. What, now, are some of the practical ways and means by which this kind of environment can be achieved?

---

* References to Dr. Blatz's security theory are made throughout the book. Sources are to be found in the bibliography.

II. THE PHYSICAL ENVIRONMENT

Space. Generally speaking, the ideal amount of outdoor space would be from seventy-five to one hundred square feet per child and indoors, forty-five to fifty-five square feet. If the areas are smaller, children feel confined and get in one another's way. On the other hand, merely increasing the space beyond these dimensions does not improve life for the children. In fact, if it becomes too large, children may feel lost in its immensity. What is more, a teacher will find that too much space makes looking after children too difficult. Adjustment of these dimensions will depend upon many things, one of which is the number of children attending the school.*

A nursery school for ten children has not the same space requirements per child as one for fifty children. Also, the ages of the children will make a difference. A school for children from two to five years must differ from one made up entirely of four-year-olds. Take for example a school where there are children from two to five years of age. They often play outdoors all together. It should be remembered that younger children usually play less actively than the older ones and there should, therefore, be enough space to allow them to play without being overwhelmed by the increasing activity of the older children. Also, the interests and skills of a two-year-old are different from those of a four-year-old; so there should be enough room for play materials and equipment to meet the interests of both age groups. This is even more important in planning the indoor play space.

Floor plan. The floor plan of a school makes a great difference in the safety, convenience and ease with which the children can find their way about. It is important to decide how the available space can best be used. For example, cloakrooms should be adjacent to the playground, and washrooms conveniently near the playrooms. Two or three playrooms should be planned so that there need not be too large a group of children in any one room.

* Ministry of Community and Social Services, Ontario, the Day Nurseries Act and Regulations, 1972:
Minimum activity room space for every child: 30 square feet of floor space and 250 cubic feet of airspace.

Convenience of furnishings. As children in a nursery school can become easily confused and bewildered, it is important that the furniture and equipment be arranged in such a way that it remains, in general, in the same position and can be found easily and used conveniently by the children. That is, in a playroom, there will be a certain corner for the blocks; a doll corner which may be fenced off from the rest of the room; a rocking chair near the bookcase; each toy in its own box and easily found on the shelves; the paint close to the painting easel.

Variety of equipment. Children should be able to change from one thing to another when they want and, of course, interests will vary with each child. Therefore, there should be a wide variety of equipment from which to choose.

Self-effort. The furniture and equipment should be designed so that a child can use them by himself. There should be small-sized tables, chairs, cupboards, toilets, washbasins. Each child should be provided with his own towel, comb, clothes cupboard, and bed. The dishes and utensils which the children use should be easy for them to manage and not easy to break.

Safety. All equipment and furnishings should be considered also in terms of safety. The outdoor play equipment must be strong, sturdy and firmly fastened down with sharp edges dulled and points rounded. Fences should be carefully designed and high enough to keep a child from climbing over. A picket fence is dangerous. It is safer if all gates have locks or catches that a teacher can open quickly and easily and that are yet well out of the children's reach. Large equipment should be spaced out so that there need not be too many children in one place at the same time. Swings need plenty of room for swinging and runways should be designed to be interesting and yet to prevent collision. Of course, it is most important to keep all equipment outdoors and indoors in good repair. Broken materials are often hazards.

Indoors, all hazards, such as windows, doors, stairs, electrical outlets, hot water taps, stoves, fireplaces, slippery floors, should be checked for safety. Sharp instruments, such as pointed scissors, knives, paper cutters, must be kept where the children can neither see nor reach them. It is a wise precaution to be sure that the paint and paste the children use is the non-poisonous kind. While it is important that the toy cupboards and bookcases be within easy reach of the children, it is equally important that the teachers' cupboards be well out of their reach.

If careful thought is given to ensuring safety, a teacher can know that she has done everything she can to keep the inevitable accidents to a minimum and also that, if they do happen, they will not be too serious. Furthermore, with careful planning for safety, she can supervise without interrupting the children too often.

Clothing. Parents can help a great deal in a nursery school's efforts to give children opportunities to do things for themselves. Often, nursery school teachers can suggest types of clothing which make it easier for a child to dress himself.

For a child to be comfortable, he needs clothes that are easy to handle. They should be warm, loose and not complicated with braces, buckles and fancy zippers. If snow suits, overalls and coats are of light weight, it is easier for a child to play; hats and helmets, of course, should be the kind that will stay comfortably and securely on the child's head. Sweaters can be of fine wool, cotton or nylon but should always be easy to put on and take off. Shoes, of course, must be large enough (how quickly they are outgrown!). Short laces avoid double knots. Canvas shoes can be used indoors to prevent slipping on the floor and to make it easier for a child to dance or skip. Mitts, not gloves, are best. The most satisfactory kind are the ones of coarsely woven wool with cuffs sewn to a long tape worn inside the coat sleeves. Leather mitts stay wet and become stiff. Fleece-lined snow boots are the warmest. A band of elastic or a strap at the top will help to keep out the snow. Everything that a child wears must be marked, of course, to avoid its getting mixed up with other children's clothing. Indoors, slacks or dresses should be loose and comfortable without belts, buckles or ties.

III. PLANNING FOR A CHILD TO LIVE AMONG
AND WITH OTHER CHILDREN

In most nursery schools, the children are divided into age groups. But, where possible, the programme will also include a time when all the children can play together. This is valuable because, in their free-choice play, the younger children learn from the older and the older ones learn to consider the younger.

Free group play. Planning for all the children to be together is most easily arranged in an outdoor playtime. Here there are many opportunities for the children to play with each other in small groups of their own choosing. It is important, therefore, to provide outdoor equipment which children can use constructively and creatively in their free group play.

Individual interests. However, play for this age should not be all group play and, therefore, the programme will include a time when, although the children are together, more emphasis is put on individual play and equipment is provided that will encourage a child's individual interests. This means that there must be enough equipment so that each child will have plenty of things to do and because, as we have said before, the skills and interests of the older children are different from those of the younger, a good arrangement is to have two playrooms indoors. The play equipment in each room can then be suited to the skills and interests of the different age groups.

Occasionally, a child will want to withdraw from the other children altogether for a little while with a book perhaps or just to look out the window. The nursery school setup should be arranged to give him this opportunity as well as the opportunity for being with the other children.

Organized group play. Children's interest in their play will be greatly stimulated if the nursery school can provide a small extra playroom or alcove to give them an opportunity to participate in "special or organized play groups." Here a teacher can take three or four children for a short time and show them what more *can* be done (never what *must* be done) with the materials they are already using every day in their free-choice play, such as paper, paste and plasticene. This little playroom or "workshop" can also be equipped with materials with which the children, under the guidance of their teacher, can experiment, construct and create: such materials as carpentry tools, clay, wood, glue and many others that a young child can use safely.

In most nursery schools, a time is also set aside for larger organized group activities, such as music, games and stories. These activities usually take place in the children's playrooms and adequate space should be arranged.

IV. THE TEACHER IS THERE

Danger. In his play, a child should feel free not only to choose what he wants to do but also to experiment as he wishes. But he may experiment to the point of danger and a teacher must be near by to caution, help, set limits and, sometimes, restrain. Too much cautioning, of course, results in one of two things. The child either pays no attention, having discovered that much of the cautioning is unnecessary, or he becomes fearful and stops experimenting altogether.

Social situations. A teacher must also always be near by to act as mediator in social situations that are getting out of hand and that the children cannot settle themselves. She can help an aggressive child modify his behaviour or she can help a timid child to stand up for himself. She can help all the children to discover that being considerate and agreeable with one another is a happier and more satisfying experience than bullying and aggression.

Every so often, a teacher will realize that the excitement of a child or a group of children is mounting too high. They may start to scream, push each other or use the equipment dangerously. By a word here and there, or a suggestion as to how to use a piece of equipment, she can often avert danger or undesirable social situations before they happen and the children are usually glad to have her support.

Setting the stage takes thought and effort by a teacher but it is of great importance because, when properly done, it provides for an easy, relaxed atmosphere with a minimum of confusion. She creates a place where children can be happy and safe; where they can be busy and active or quiet and relaxed. She provides a place where they can learn to enjoy being with others of their own age; a place where they have an opportunity to start learning constructive and creative play habits; a place where they will slowly grow in independence and responsibility.

4. Helping a child fit into a way of living

All groups of human beings have their own ways of doing things. In our cities, for instance, we stop our cars when the red light is on and move ahead when it turns green. This way of working out traffic movements is written down and defined for us as a law or a regulation. There are a great many practices which, although they are not formal regulations, most of us accept and carry out because we are members of a particular society, such as eating our dinner with a fork rather than our hands, and wearing a tie to a formal dining room.

Folkways and mores. Social scientists talk about these habits as the folkways and mores of a group and they have shown us how these serve to hold a group together and strengthen it. Also they have shown us how they are useful to an individual person in helping him fit in as a member of his social group. We are told that every society has its plan by which its young come to accept its folkways and mores and, through their assimilation of these, to become integrated as members into that society.

28

Naturally these folkways and mores curtail, to some extent, our personal ways of doing things and many adults in our modern world have come to think of them as designed to annoy them. Much is being said and written about society *versus* the individual and about the individual *versus* society.

Yet, there is another way of thinking about our patterns of social living and that is that our folkways and mores and regulations are established, not to impede us, but really to let each of us achieve more efficiently what we need as individuals and still have the support and enjoyment of group living. Certainly, the red light stops us when we are in a hurry to get to work but, without signals, there would be such a jam of traffic that no one would get through for hours. In other words, traffic regulations help us rather than hinder us. So, too, do a good many of our social customs. Our simple way of saying, "How do you do?" when we meet an acquaintance gives us a conventional *entrée* into conversation that both of us understand. A society that lacked these customary ways of doing things would be one of total confusion. Indeed part of the confusion of our world in the 1970's may well be attributed to the breakdown in previously established folkways and mores and no substitution of these by more appropriate ones.

Of course, mores and folkways need to be changed when they no longer apply in a changing society, otherwise they do begin to impede individuals. In particular, some people have felt that social regulations interfered with a young child's development as an individual. This approach grows out of the early psychological thinking, stimulated by Freud. Particular concern was expressed regarding the pressures which social customs put on the lives of children. And, if we think back to the Victorian age, it is easy to see this was quite correct, for, in those days, children were "to be seen and not heard." Their needs for running, jumping and playing were suppressed as quickly as possible and they were expected to conform to correct adult forms of behaviour.

We know now that a child should not be expected to accept adult forms of behaviour all at once. We know that he must learn them gradually as his understanding increases and his need for group living expands. We believe that, properly introduced to them, a child can learn to appreciate the folkways and mores of his society.

A good approach would be to try to accomplish two things at the same time: one, to help the children learn the nursery school's "folkways, mores and laws" by which they are going to live; two, by setting these to meet the children's needs and capacities, to help them realize that such patterns are set for their benefit and are not obstacles devised to impede them.

Requirements. Nursery schools, of course, do not talk of these things as folkways and mores, law and authority. They are referred to as "requirements." They might also be called rules and regulations, limits or boundaries. It is completely impossible for a nursery school, or any other organization, to exist without requirements. Schools do vary, however, in the extent to which they are aware of what requirements they are using. Indeed, it is often the school which states that it has no requirements at all that actually uses the most and, because it is not clear as to what it does require, children are confused as to what is expected of them. How oblivious adults can be to the requirements they actually make is shown in this true and revealing anecdote. A visitor asked a nursery school teacher, "What are your rules with regard to the sandbox?" The teacher answered, "Horrors, we have no rules in this school!" "What do you do, then, when a child throws sand?" the visitor asked. "Oh, they're not allowed to do that," was the answer.

We believe that the requirements of nursery school living can be such that they will enhance rather than impede the life of a child. He will discover that certain ways of doing things may restrict him from acting on every temporary impulse but that, through them, his needs will be taken care of and that opportunities to achieve his own goals will be plentiful

We believe, however, that there should not be more requirements than are necessary and that these few should be well defined. It is most important to be aware of what is really being required of a child and why.

It is important for a nursery school to examine its programmes and procedures carefully to ascertain just what requirements are being made and to check that additional requirements are not being brought in surreptitiously. Requirements of which the staff are unwitting may seriously interfere with the children's freedom.

The daily programme for a nursery school child is made up, more or less, of routine periods and play periods. In both these periods, there are certain things which can and others which cannot be done by the children: in other words there are certain requirements of behaviour which we want the children to accept. The teacher makes these requirements to meet each child's needs and also because she realizes that, in any group living, an individual must learn to regulate his behaviour. Therefore, when she presents the requirements to him, she should feel confident that they are suitable for his well-being and necessary for the group. It thus becomes a teacher's responsibility first to decide *what* requirements there should be in the daily procedure and then to teach these to the children, in such a way that they will come to enjoy accepting them rather than doing what is required of them only because they have to do what the teacher tells them.

Very often, a child is negative and resistant because he does not understand what is expected of him. So, if a teacher is confident that certain requirements are necessary, why not let the children be aware of this too? After all, the children themselves will later have to take such a responsibility for themselves.

When a teacher asks and expects a child to accept these requirements, she must show him how they can be carried out in a way that will be worthwhile to him. For example, outdoors a child should be able to climb if he wants to. But in order that no harm may come to him he is required to climb on the jungle gym and not on the fence. A child should be comfortably dressed. Therefore, in winter, he is required to wear his coat if he wants to go out. If the requirements are properly presented, a child soon comes to realize that his acceptance of them will be a satisfaction to himself. Some children, of course, find this out more quickly than others.

II. GENERAL PRINCIPLES IN SETTING UP REQUIREMENTS

Of course, the way in which requirements are set up and the ways in which they are carried out will vary considerably with different groups of children and in different nursery schools. But in establishing any requirements, there are general principles to keep in mind.

Characteristics. Requirements have the following characteristics: as *few* as possible and *necessary; clearly defined* and *obviously reasonable; consistently* asked and consistently carried out; of *interest* to a child and within his capacity to fulfil.

Sometimes, adults require many unnecessary things of children. For instance, when a child is playing in the sand, he can be required to keep from throwing the sand at another child but should not be required to keep his coat clean. A child can be required to use his spoon instead of his fingers but should not be required to hold his spoon as an adult would. In the sleeping room, a child can be required to lie on his bed but should not be required to lie on his face if he prefers to be on his side. A good motto for nursery school teachers might be, "Is this requirement really necessary?"

The requirements that *are* asked should be obviously reasonable. For instance, "It is time to wash your hands because dinner is nearly ready." "Drink up your milk so that you can go into the playroom." The more obvious the reason behind a requirement, the more likely a child will be to accept it. However, explanation of requirements to children can be greatly overdone. Most children are quick to become aware of the reason behind them, and then little or no explanation is necessary.

All requirements should be asked consistently so that a child will come to realize there is no doubt or uncertainty about them. He will not think, "I wonder if I have to do this today?"

Most important of all is that a teacher be sure that what she is requiring of a child is within his capacity to fulfil. How futile to ask a child to take his snow boots off when they are too tight, or to say to him, "It's time to go to sleep now," when perhaps he may not be able to sleep.

Adults often make impossible requirements of children. Everyone has heard of incidents like the following. A mother holds her young daughter in her arms to show her to Aunt Mary who has come to call. "Say hello to Aunt Mary," the mother says, "Say hello—can't you say hello?" smiling apologetically at Aunt Mary, who is doing her part by saying self-consciously "Hello, hello." The child, like Br'er Rabbit, says absolutely nothing—as a matter of fact, she hasn't yet learned to talk!

There are a great many things that we, as adults, can do to make it easier for a child to accept requirements. If he is interested in what he is doing, he will learn more quickly. Having his own cupboard, his own towel and comb, helping himself to fruit juice will give him the thrill of doing things for himself and he will accept happily what has to be done. We can also make it easier for him by varying the detail of a requirement: if he does not like juice, the amount offered to him could be much smaller than the usual quantity.

Games. There are, of course, many other ways that are used by different people to get a child to do what he has to do. Some of these are devices which seem to involve fooling a child. They sabotage the trust that is developing between child and adult, for they obviate frankness and straight-forwardness. One of these devices that is used quite frequently is to make a game out of everything that has to be done. Games are far too important to be used in this subversive fashion. Besides that, the adult is put in the difficult position of having continually to improve the game as time goes on. For instance, in some nursery school cloakrooms, each child's shoes go in the top of his cupboard. A teacher might say: "Here are your shoes—let us pretend they are a pair of bunnies and they are going to jump *right* into this little hole!!! Here they go—here they go—Whoops—*there* they are!" This is fun, of course, but on Monday she tells of bunnies, on Tuesday of birds and, on Wednesday, may have run out of ideas or be just too tired to go on inventing anyway. Nowadays, there are even toy trains to persuade children to eat. As the train is put on the table, the coal car has the meat, the baggage car the potato, on down to the dessert in the caboose!

And how often do we hear of coaxing games such as this: "Come on now, let the scrambled eggs go down the little red lane to play with the beans."

These games may be fun for the moment, but if a child is really to learn to put his shoes in his own cupboard, requirements which follow the general principles outlined above will in the long run be more effective than a game. The task is obviously within the child's capacity. It is reasonable and the teacher can be consistent in what she is asking him to do.

III. REQUIREMENTS IN DIFFERENT PARTS OF
NURSERY SCHOOL LIFE

IN PLAY

In nursery school play periods, a teacher wants each child to be free to choose for himself, to have his own ideas and to experiment as he will. Therefore, as we have said before, when she sets the stage she must make sure it is as safe as possible so that each child can have this freedom.

Safety. Even so, there are necessary safety rules which a child of this age must learn. For instance, sand cannot be thrown at another child. A slide is too steep to walk up; so the steps should be used. A see-saw should not bump on the ground because a child might be jolted off. Paint and paste must not be eaten. Once a child has learned and accepted these rules, adults will not need to interrupt his activity and actually he can then be even freer in his play.

Destruction. Most nursery schools are confronted with a budget, and destructive play would soon result in no more equipment. A child can quickly learn that if he wishes to use something he must try to use it so that it will not be destroyed. In these days when natural resources are being depleted and conservation has become all important, a child cannot begin too young to learn to take care of equipment and materials so he can have the enjoyment of using them again.

Of course most young children enjoy breaking things down as much as they enjoy building them up. It doesn't matter whether the source of this "breaking downness" is to be attributed to some deep feeling in a child or whether it is considered an ordinary activity that grows out of a child's desire to experiment with the world around him. Nevertheless, to think that children must be given opportunities for breaking furniture and damaging equipment seems rather ridiculous. Actually, the play materials in a well-equipped nursery school provide plenty of legitimate opportunities for children to pull things apart. They can get as much fun out of taking down a colour-cone as out of breaking a chair. They can express themselves by putting paint on paper just as adequately as by putting paint on the walls. The requirement for well children is that they use the proper places and the proper media for such expression.

Time and place. Certain rules of time and place are necessary: sand is played with in the sandbox; scissors are to be used only while sitting at a table; the *teacher* decides when it is the right time for a child to go indoors. At first, it might be difficult for a child to understand the reason for such rules as these. But, if he has trust in the adult he soon accepts them as being a perfectly natural way of doing things and just part of the regular course of events.

IN ROUTINE

Order. The requirements of safety, care of equipment, and attention to time and place will be necessary in routine activities as well as in play. With routines, we can add the requirement of following a flexible but consistent order of procedure. For example, a child will be required to take off his outdoor clothes when he plays indoors; he will rinse his fingers after going to the toilet; he will have his dinner at a certain hour; he will sit at the table to eat and have his first course before his dessert.

Actually, even a more or less definite order of taking off his outdoor clothing might be expected of a child because this has proved to be a convenient way for him to undress. For instance, he may start with his hat, scarf or mitts, next his coat, then, sitting down on the floor, remove his snow suit and shoes; he will reverse this order when getting dressed to go outdoors. Once a child has shown a willingness to accept the requirements in general and is beginning to share the responsibility for carrying them out with his teacher, naturally, the smaller details of how he dresses and undresses can be left to him. They will vary with each child: for instance, one child may like to put his hat away in his pocket while another likes to put it in the cupboard, or a child may one day like to take off his coat first and on the next day his hat.

Variation of requirement. In all requirements, the small details can usually be left to the child. For instance, at dinner, one child may like to use his spoon, another his fork; one child may eat slowly, another quickly; at nap time, one child may like to pull the blankets up to his face, another to push them down.

Gradual presentation. Naturally, when a child first comes to school, he is not immediately faced with a lot of requirements! His teacher takes the full responsibility for anything that has to be done. She lets him do as little or as much as he wants to and in the way he wants to do it. For instance, a child may, at first, like to sleep with his shoes on. He might want to sit on a teacher's lap for his dinner. He may not want to wash his hands at all. Little by little, the teacher will make him aware of what is expected of him. But she will make the early requirements a very small part indeed of what he will be expected to do later on. For example, one new little girl at first refused to drink her fruit juice. For a day or two, the teacher required only that she have a drink of water instead. In a few days, a very little juice was added. She accepted this and discovered she liked it if it was mixed with water. So, for several days, she helped herself to two glasses and mixed the juice and water back and forth to her liking!! Soon she was too busy to bother and drank it willingly as it was offered to her.

IN SOCIAL ACTIVITIES OF ROUTINES AND PLAY

A teacher knows that when a group of children are together, they will learn a great deal from one another. For instance, if a child tries to take another child's toy, he discovers that the other child does not like it and pushes him away. If a child is determined always to have *his own* way, the other children may not want to play with him and he will learn a great deal from this experience. But a teacher needs to lay down certain requirements of behaviour as well, which will help a child in his social relationships. A child should learn that hitting, pushing and bullying are not accepted ways of playing and he can be required to play without engaging in them. He can be required to consider other children's rights. For instance, a child cannot be permitted to push another child out of the swing. He cannot be permitted to knock down another child's house of blocks. In periods of routine children are usually together in small groups; here too, they can be required to consider one another's rights and keep from disturbing one another.

Certain requirements of behaviour will help a child discover that being generally agreeable makes for happier relations all round, not only with his own companions but with adults too. Some children constantly demand attention from an adult by whining and complaining, "I don't want this" and "I don't want that." A child should never get what he wants by whining. Naturally, a teacher understands that perhaps a child is tired and feels cross and irritable but she can also help him, through the proper use of requirements, to learn that other forms of behaviour are better.

When a child is having unusual difficulty in fitting in with the other children, his teacher will review his development as a whole. The cause of the difficulty is usually found to lie in another area of his adjustment. This discovery will help her to decide how much she should be requiring of him and what she should do to help him. It is important to point out here again that learning does not take place all at once. It might be many months before a child learns new forms of behaviour.

IV. VERBAL DIRECTION

Having set up requirements for a child a teacher now becomes responsible for helping him become aware of what they are and for showing him how to carry them out. She must direct the child as he is learning.

Some teachers shy away from the word direction and, of course, over-direction is to be avoided. But the definition of direction is "to regulate the course of; to guide, conduct and to advise," and surely a pre-school child needs this attention. He has lived only two or three years and he cannot possibly know what should and should not be done. Therefore, the teacher must consider *how much* direction she should give, *when* to give it and *how* to give it.

The amount of direction varies with each child because each child will learn at his own rate. For example, Mary, a two-year-old, has always had a great deal done for her, has little or no interest and very little skill. Her teacher will have to give her a lot of help and direction to start with and will require of her very, very little. John, on the other hand, is a quiet and eager learner, has interest and skill. His teacher can expect him to take more responsibility and she can reduce her direction to a minimum.

In a new situation, a child does not know what is expected of him. Naturally, his teacher will inform him about this and give him a few simple reasons to help him understand. But most adults talk far too much. They forget that, given half a chance, young children learn very quickly and that, furthermore, most of them remember better than some adults do! Once a child understands the requirements of the procedure, he should be given a chance to remember them for himself without unnecessary repetition of explanation and reasoning, which may only induce the child to argue. It is all too easy for an adult to enter into a mutual argument which so often ends in mutual irritation as well.

Method. A good method of giving direction and one that a child seems to accept very readily is, first, to gain a child's attention by a word or touch or even to take him by the hand. Then, when he is listening, give the direction clearly and simply so that he understands and is ready to think what he is going to do. This method can be applied not only with an individual child but also in situations where a teacher has to control and direct a group as a whole.

It is better not to phrase a direction as though it were a personal request to a child but, rather, to give it in the form of *information* or a statement of fact such as, "Your shoes go in the top of your cupboard," or "It's time to get washed," or "You may go inside now Peter." This immediately gives the child a chance to share with the teacher the responsibility of carrying out the requirement. As a child grows older and becomes familiar with the procedure, the direction can be phrased as a *question*: "Where do your shoes go?" "Have you had your fruit juice?" "Which is your bed?" "What do you do next?" Perhaps in some cases a mere *suggestion* will be enough: handing a child his shoes or saying only "Your shoes." It is much safer *not* to say, "Would you like to come and get washed now?" The child might very well answer, "No thank you very much," and the teacher will be in a terrible dilemma!

It is wise not to use any certain form of direction too often. For instance, asking a child "Can you manage?" may start off by being a useful and natural question, but if it is used too much it not only loses its meaning but becomes silly in its very monotony. Again, the form of direction used must make sense. For example, saying to a child "We put the toys on the shelf" may give information but the direction would be better if phrased, "The toys go on the shelf" or "Let me show you where the toys go." Using "we" inappropriately can lead a teacher into a silly position: for instance, it does not make sense to say to a child, "We don't run in the halls" or "We don't hit each other" when he has just done this. A teacher might, on the other hand, say, "Come along, we are all going to dinner now," and here "we" would be used appropriately. It is important to watch that our phraseology does not become stereotyped.

Commands such as "Put your shoes in the cupboard because that's where they go," "Wash your hands because they are dirty," phrase directions in a more clearly defined manner. These can be called informative *commands*. They are clear and to the point and easily understood. Once a child is familiar with the procedures and has shown a willingness to accept them, he may appreciate this form of direction more than a lot of unnecessary discussion and explanation. However, as we have said, giving direction as information permits a child to feel a share in the responsibility, whereas a command leaves him with little or no responsibility. Therefore, a wise teacher will not use commands too often. When they *are* used, they must not, nor do they need to, sound overbearing, or as if the teacher were ordering the children about.

A *positive form* of direction, rather than a negative one, has an astonishing effect on a young child and he will accept the direction much more readily—"Do this," instead of "Don't do that,"—"You must keep the blocks on the floor, John," instead of "Don't throw the blocks." However, as with every other form of direction suggested, the recommendation to use a positive form must not be followed too literally. For instance, an adult will often say quite naturally "Don't forget your hat" or "Don't be upset, everything will be all right."

The form of direction a teacher uses will depend, a great deal, on the attitude of the child. This will vary with different children. If a child has learned to trust the teacher and is eager to do what is required of him, a mere suggestion, if any, is all that will be necessary, whereas another child may respond only to a clearer and much more definite form of direction. Occasionally, a child has formed a habit of protesting and arguing about everything. The teacher would be wise to direct this child in such a way as to avoid argument, that is, with a minimum of explanation or discussion.

If this plan of giving direction is sensibly and consistently carried out, as outlined, a child comes to have confidence in the requirements and also to trust and respect the authority of the adult who gives them. Then, when a situation arises in which a child can be given no responsibility at all, such as fire drill, or when he is about to run out on the street in front of a car, and the teacher directs with a straight command, he will trust her and obey.

A teacher's voice. In helping a child develop an attitude of acceptance towards what has to be done, a teacher's voice plays a very important part.

A teacher's voice should be natural, not affected or artificial. It should be pleasant and kind, neither too loud nor too soft. Whispering makes her sound silly. When a teacher knows she has something to say that a child should hear, she should speak with a tone of definite assurance in her voice and showing no doubt or uncertainty in her attitude. She should speak clearly and to the point. She will try not to sound complaining or annoyed. She will not talk down to a child, gush or use "baby talk," but speak in an ordinary tone of voice, as one person to another.

A teacher must beware of making too obvious an effort to speak to a child "just in the right way." This immediately creates an artificial situation. We have described one way of speaking to children in this chapter, but this should be thought of as a guide only. The most important thing of all for a teacher to remember is to speak naturally and with a relaxed manner. Working together and sharing the responsibility of carrying out the requirements can be a wonderful experience for both adult and child and, if a teacher is relaxed and enjoying herself, the child will know this by her tone of voice. He, too, will relax and enjoy life under her direction.

A teacher's attitude. A teacher wants a child to learn to accept the necessary requirements, knowing that he will find them worthwhile and useful to him. She can help him to do this by her own attitude. If he is to believe in the requirements, she must believe in them too. She wants him to work busily and get ahead, and so she herself must be businesslike. She wants him to enjoy his activity; she herself must therefore show a real interest and enjoyment in what they are doing together. She wants him to be proud of what he can do and so she will encourage him and approve of his efforts.

A teacher may feel very concerned about a certain child who is having difficulty in one of his learning situations, but she does not want him to worry and become anxious. So, with him, she is always particularly relaxed and easy, not overserious or grim. She will show understanding of the child's immaturity and failures, and never be sarcastic or ridicule him.

As she interprets the requirements to a child, she will expect his attention and acceptance, knowing that her authority and control stem from the knowledge that the requirements are wise and not from a feeling of personal power. Above all, she will help a child realize that the requirement is not just a personal whim, but something that is necessary to do, and that they are going to carry it out *together*.

In summarizing, we repeat that we believe certain requirements should be set up for a pre-school child, because they are necessary for his existence and well-being. We believe that they should be well defined in order to make it easy for a child to become aware of them. The *method* a teacher uses to present the requirements to the children and the *way* she gives her direction and help cannot be stressed too strongly because these are the important factors in helping a child to be happy in his acceptance of the requirements. They are also the important factors in helping a child discover the thrill of slowly taking responsibility himself, while he continues to be content under the dependable and just control of adults.

5.   Helping a child accept dependence

I. HELP

Parents, teachers and psychologists have put so much emphasis on a child's learning to do things on his own that they sometimes forget how important it is that he also learn to accept help. None of us, child or adult, can exist without people to help us. Every time we attack tasks that are difficult, we need help. Every time we are inadequate to deal with situations, perhaps through illness or crises, other people must step in to assist us. We are indeed dependent upon other people, as they are on us. Our dependency takes at least two forms: one, a need for other people to assist us in some understanding—this assistance we can call *help*; and two, a need for people to bolster us, as it were, when we feel inadequate or discouraged—this aid we can call *support*. To learn to accept both help with a task and support is extremely important.

Necessity. The more responsibility a person assumes, the more he is dependent upon the help and support of other people. Unfortunately, children have too often been trained to feel that to be dependent and to accept help is undesirable; hence many adults who are actually greatly dependent on others do not recognize and even deny this fact. The extreme of this denial of dependence is reflected in our popular phrases: "a self-made man"; "He pulled himself up by his own boot-straps"; or "he made his own way in the world." These descriptions are never true. Indeed, a man who is the head of a large organization is dependent on the help of his employees and colleagues, as well as on the support of his friends and family. If he is unaware of, or unwilling to admit this, he carries an excess weight of self-importance and self-responsibility which may be a source of one of the many illnesses attributed glibly to "the stress and strain of modern living." The willingness to accept the fact of one's dependence is necessary for the psychological health of anyone living in a human society. Whether a person is baking a cake or devising a new political programme, he cannot do it entirely by himself. For his cake, he is dependent on the farmer who grew the wheat and the electrician who installed the stove, as well as upon the immediate people whom he may request to bring him the butter or to keep out from underfoot.

Efficiency. Accepting help is not only necessary; it is an efficient way of living. A person in a strange city who refuses to ask directions wastes a great deal of time. The person who cannot open his garage doors and is too stubborn to ask his neighbour to give him a hand is wasting considerable energy. Yet, there are a great many people who determinedly refuse to ask for help.

Then, too, there are many tasks that one person can do only with difficulty but that can easily be done by two or more people. In a psychological experiment, a problem situation was arranged in which a child had to move certain objects from one room to another. It was difficult, almost impossible, to get the objects through the door and, at the same time, keep the door open. The children who solved the problem most quickly were those who realized that the answer was to call another child and ask him to hold the door while they dealt with the package.

Enjoyment. However, accepting help is more than necessary and efficient; it is also enjoyable. It is a way of expressing our relationship with other people. How often we say "May I help you?" or "Let me do that for you." The individuals could obviously do these things for themselves, but human relationship is expressed pleasantly and courteously through our offer.

Often, it is simply more fun to carry out a task with other people than to do it by oneself. To work with others, whether in cooking supper at a campfire or in writing a book, enhances the activity. So often adults deny themselves this great pleasure by a tremendous drive to demonstrate that they are capable of doing such things by themselves.

Willingness to accept help. Some people may suppose that a child does not have to *learn* to accept help because, ever since he was an infant, he has been accepting it of necessity. But children may learn to resist help, even from their parents, if they are made to feel that they should do without it as soon as possible. There is some indication that children can be divided into two groups: those who reject adult help when it is necessary, that is, when they can't do what they are trying to do by themselves; and those who accept it. Preliminary research from studies by Dorothy Keschner and Carroll Davis (see bibliography) shows that children who are willing to accept help when they need it are more mentally healthy than those who resist it. They are certainly more sensible.

Nursery schools may well provide the crucial point at which a child's attitude towards accepting help is established. Teachers may be able to assist him to learn that to accept the help and support of adults is necessary, efficient and enjoyable, and that the greater the extent to which he makes use of available help, the greater will be his capacity for going ahead and doing things by himself.

II. PHYSICAL DIRECTION

One of the first ways of giving children a chance to accept help is by making them feel comfortable in taking what we call direction. This direction can be either verbal, *telling* a child what to do, or physical, *showing* a child what to do. In chapter 4 we discussed ways of giving verbal direction but with a younger nursery school child physical direction is probably more important than verbal. The following example will show the importance of it. A few years ago, ten children were divided into two groups of five. Each group was to learn the washroom procedure, which consisted of ten consecutive steps. The first group was taught by verbal direction only. The second group was *shown* how and helped without any verbal direction at all. The second group learned more quickly than the first group.

It is very easy to get into the habit of giving too many verbal directions. There is a great danger of fussing over and bothering children; of being "at them" all the time; of nagging. Giving too many verbal directions usually results in one of two things: a child rebels or he becomes clever at paying no attention at all. Very often, *showing* a child what he is expected to do and helping him do it, with very little or no talk, is the best way to teach him.

In routines. In the past so much emphasis has been put on a child's becoming independent and responsible and learning to choose for himself, that adults have felt they should drop out of the picture as soon as possible. However, there has been a tendency to do this too soon.

Let us use the dressing and undressing routine as an example. To be sure, the ultimate aim is that a child assume responsibility and become skilful enough to be able to dress and undress himself. But as children are going to get dressed and undressed several times a day for seventy-five years, what is the hurry? Learning to take full responsibility for a task may be spread over a period of many years.

Most young children like to start helping themselves and, of course, we must take advantage of this interest, as it is through doing things for themselves that they gradually become skilful. However, physical skill is not the only thing to be learned by children. Paying attention to what they are doing and getting ahead without playing or disturbing other children are just as important in a child's learning as becoming skilful. A young child's span of attention is not yet sufficiently developed to allow him to work at a task for more than a few minutes at a time, and if too much is expected of him and he is allowed too much time for self-help he is almost sure to get into habits of dawdling and playing and disturbing others. Perhaps he will start to worry about his responsibilities or become negative and emotional through trying to do something that is too hard for him. In a nursery school cloakroom, a teacher should give enough help to keep this from happening. Occasionally, a child who has been expected to become independent too soon will be suspicious and antagonistic towards a teacher instead of trustful and happy in his dependence on her. By her attitude and by the way she gives help and direction, a teacher can, little by little, dispel these unfortunate attitudes and slowly build up more desirable ones. A good nursery school teacher will consider this one of her most important responsibilities.

From the beginning of this particular routine, however, the teacher should assume that the task is the child's and that she is helping *him*. She will say to him, "May I help you?" rather than "You help *me*." Thus the child will begin to feel that dressing and undressing are eventually to become his own responsibility. Of course, there are occasions when a child can be expected to help an adult with *her* responsibilities, such as setting the table or doing simple errands. Then the adult can properly say "Thank you very much for helping *me*." Even when a child is very young, he can discover the pleasure of doing things for other people.

When a new child comes to school, he needs a great deal of help with almost everything, particularly with dressing and undressing, and so, while his teacher expects him to watch and pay attention, she will do nearly all of the job herself. At first he will be expected only to put his hat in his cupboard or get his snow boots so that his teacher can put them on, or try to put on one shoe while his teacher does the other. Little by little he will be expected to do more as he becomes more skilful.

Although a child can be expected gradually to do more for himself his teacher will, throughout the nursery school years, give help with zippers and buckles, shoe-laces and snow boots, and hanging up clothes in cupboards. And why not? Even adults get pleasure out of helping each other on and off with their coats and, as an adult helps a child in his tasks, both of them can enjoy the experience. This relationship is valuable indeed for a child.

In play. In play periods, the same plan of giving help can be followed. Leading a child by the hand, carrying him, restraining him from danger, will help him to learn the necessary boundaries of his play better than many verbal directions. Again, the amount of help varies with each child. Some may depend on the teacher too much; others may become too independent. We want a child to feel free to choose what he wants to do in his play but, sometimes, he may not know what to do or what to choose. Here again, the teacher should join in, helping him to discover the exciting possibilities of his play equipment and materials.

Touch. In giving verbal directions, a teacher is aware of her tone of voice. In giving physical directions, she must be aware of how she guides and helps a child. Her touch should be sure, yet gentle. She will lead a child by the hand, *not by the wrist.* When restraining a child she will help, not force him, and will be careful not to move too suddenly. When she carries a child, she will carry him so that he feels comfortable and safe. As in giving verbal directions, before she shows a child how to do something, she will gain his attention and have him watch what she is doing. This is particularly important in dressing and washing. So often, an adult will dress a child as fast as she can just to get it over with, while the child is standing passively, thinking of something else altogether. If a child loses interest and starts to play or talk so much that he forgets what he is doing, the teacher should stop helping him, recall his attention and then start again. If a child is watching, he is usually learning.

The role of an adult with any child is that of teacher and it is through teaching that a child will learn. At first, a nursery school teacher assumes full responsibility but as she helps a child learn, very slowly she expects him to assume his share of responsibility and do more for himself.

Through a child's routines, a teacher is helping the child to develop skill, to pay attention to what he is doing and to have fun doing it. In his play, she is helping him learn to choose what he wants to do; to experiment and to create on his own; she will, therefore, encourage him to have his own ideas and to try things for himself. But she also wants him to enjoy help and to be willing to accept other people's ideas, and so she will often unobtrusively join in his activities. A teacher must always be careful, however, to accept a child's own standards of achievement.

As she teaches, she will be serious, yet relaxed; she will help, not criticize; she will always be interested but will not fuss or bother the children. Thus, the children will be happy and contented in their dependence on the teacher as they slowly learn.

III. HELP FOR A CHILD WHO CRIES

Nursery school teachers often hear a parent or visitor say, "Don't your children ever cry? I haven't heard a single child crying!" Actually, it is amazing how little crying there is in a busy, happy nursery school. Of course, sometimes children do cry and, when they do, a teacher should know how she can best be of aid to them.

Crying is a signal that human beings use to indicate that they need help. When adults cry, and they do, it is usually because life has become too much for them; some situation has unduly frightened or angered them; they feel inadequate, grieved, desolate or frustrated, and they are really asking for support. Adults are usually able to suppress their crying and children are taught, at a very early age, to try to do the same. However, perhaps too much emphasis has been put on teaching children to control their crying; actually it is a natural physiological reaction (which, interestingly enough, occurs only in human beings). It indicates a state of "insecurity" which can be remedied by the acceptance of a "dependent security". With nursery school children, we accept the fact that crying means a signal for help.

A new child. It is hard for a great many children, when they first come to nursery school, to say goodbye to their parents. A child feels strange and is usually a little fearful to have his mother leave him, even if he has learned to hide his feelings. His teacher understands that this is the most natural thing in the world and she will do everything in her power to protect and reassure him. She will be ready with a plan to help him. She may lead him by the hand or even carry him. She may let him "just watch" what is going on around him, or divert him by playing *with* him in the sandbox or showing him picture books. At mealtime and rest time, she will be close to him or even have him on her lap. Soon he no longer feels strange; he begins to feel happy and his crying stops. Sometimes, even after a child is happy at school, he may arrive in the morning irritable and tearful. His teacher must remember that this, too, is natural enough. Perhaps, however, she could let him play inside by himself or with a teacher until he feels better. Or, he might cheer up more quickly by going out to play with his friends right away. The cause of this kind of crying is usually something that has happened at home and, once at school, a child soon becomes interested in his school activities. It should also be remembered that some children appear more serious than others even when they are quite content. Neither children nor adults feel like smiling or laughing all the time.

A hurt child. Usually when a child cries in the nursery school, it is because he has hurt himself. Children of this age like to run and skip from place to place and, of course, sometimes they fall or bump into something. They may pinch their fingers when they are building with blocks or drop one on their toes or perhaps fall off a tricycle. Everything in a nursery school is arranged to be as safe as possible for the children but even so these little accidents do occur. Some adults feel that they can help a child to be brave by saying, "Oh, that doesn't hurt" (when it probably really does). But there can be too little sympathy. When a child is hurt, his teacher should be infinitely sympathetic; she will console and reassure. She may say, "I know that *does* hurt, but try to stop crying and let's go and get a handkerchief." Or she might say, "Would you like to sit here with me for a little while?" Or she might divert the child by saying, "Let's go over to the sandbox and watch what the other children are doing." Or she might suggest that they get a bandage. Even when bandaging is not really necessary, it is a good thing to do. The children come to like putting on a bandage and then, when first aid *is* necessary, a child will accept it much more readily and will not likely be as frightened of it.

A child who cries for attention. However, a child may cry when he is not really hurt at all and if his teacher fusses over him too much he may soon discover that this is a good way to get attention! When he falls, he may just lie on the ground and wait for a teacher to rush over and pick him up. The teacher can help him learn to look after himself and to take these little falls without always crying, not by teasing or scolding him, but by saying something like, "Are you all right?" or "Up you get, there is no need to be upset," then "You had better go more slowly next time."

Of course, a child who cries for attention may be one who wants more help and support from adults than he is getting. When children cry a good deal, it may be wise to see that during their other activities, they are getting the help, support and reassurance that they need. Such a child might be the one who sits beside the teacher in the music circle or who is shown a little extra interest in the house he is building. He may be trying to do too much on his own and attempting things that are too difficult for him. His teacher may need to give him more help in choosing his activities.

A child who is upset by other children. Sometimes a child will cry when he cannot get what he wants from the other children; he may, for instance, want to join a group activity and the other children don't accept him. It is not wise for a teacher to insist that the other children include him; it would be better for her to try to interest him, for the time being, in something else. Situations of this sort often occur in a nursery school and usually are not serious. However, if the same child were often excluded his teacher would try to find out why the other children did not want to play with him. Perhaps he does not know *how* to play. The teacher can help him develop more skill with his play materials. Perhaps he has not learned how to play with a group of other children. The teacher can help him there too. She may start to build a sand castle or a snowman with him and soon two or three other children will want to join in and play with *him*. Teacher and children can play together for a little while and, before long, the teacher can drop out.

A child may cry if he has to wait for his turn on the swing or because he can't have the tricycle that some other child is riding. Again the teacher will explain: "Don't worry. You can have it as soon as John is finished with it." She will then help him find something to do while he is waiting. A nursery school child usually cannot understand taking turns so the teacher must be the one to decide whose turn it is to be.

A sick or tired child. Occasionally, a child cries for no apparent reason. In this case, he may be tired or even not feeling very well.

Naturally, it is up to his teacher to find out what is making him cry, if she can, and act accordingly. She might telephone his mother to find out if anything unusual could have upset him before he came to school. In the meantime, knowing that his crying is a sign of some kind of uneasiness, she might tell him a story or help him choose a favourite toy or let him just watch the other children.

A child who cries in his sleep. Once in a while, a child will cry out in his sleep and wake up frightened and crying. It is impossible to ascertain the specific cause of this behaviour. It may be a response to a dream situation or to a feeling of strangeness on waking. When this kind of crying occurs, the teacher should quickly go to the child to reassure him; she might sit him up or lift him in her arms for a few moments. He will probably drop off to sleep again but the teacher may decide that it is better for him to get up.

Noises. All nursery school teachers know that sudden or loud noises, such as the fire bell or thunder, may be frightening to small children. A nursery school teacher can help a child with these. She can prepare him for fire bells and thunder by explanation ahead of time, perhaps in story form, and thus help him to understand them. An anecdote of a nursery school child who showed her fear of thunder will illustrate. Her teacher taught her a song about thunderstorms which the child liked very much, and one day when there was a storm while she was in the sleeping room the song helped her overcome her fear. Nearly everyone else was asleep, but this little girl sat up and, in a loud stage whisper, said, quite happily, "Miss Brown, would it be all right if I sang the thunderstorm song?"

Strange costumes. On such occasions as Hallowe'en or Christmas, children are sometimes frightened and will cry when they see a dressed-up clown with a funny mask, or Santa Claus in his red suit and cap.

Here again, a teacher can prepare a child by letting him see the costumes and perhaps showing how another child can get dressed in funny clothes. If the teacher will take the trouble to do this ahead of time, the child will not be fearful on the occasion but instead will probably laugh with delight.

Animals. Some children have not had an opportunity to become accustomed to dogs or cats and they will cry when one comes near them. Children who are afraid of animals miss so much fun that teachers should do everything they can to help them overcome this fear. Stories and pictures are useful, and real dogs or kittens might even be brought into the school. A frightened child can sit on a teacher's lap at first, then, little by little, come closer, perhaps even to "touch the kitten." A teacher should never force a child or tease him but gradually help him to become familiar with what is frightening him.

Sometimes, if a child is frightened of animals, it is a help to him if a teacher can show him how *he* must be careful and gentle with *animals*. Children will be fascinated to learn how to watch birds and squirrels: to learn to "stand quite still and be perfectly quiet so as not to frighten them." It is a good thing to teach children that even worms must be handled gently. When a child digs up a worm in the garden, he may be thrilled and excited, want to hurt or kill it, or perhaps be frightened of it. His teacher should show him how to handle it gently, dig a new hole for it and let it go into the ground again! Naturally, she herself will try to show neither fear nor dislike since children of this age will imitate adults. Some teachers will learn as much as the children!

Unusual reasons. Very occasionally, a child will cry for unusual reasons. When Peter aged three, first came to school, he would appear frightened, run to the teacher and cry whenever he saw *another* child fall down. He also cried when he saw a child drop his dinner plate. The teacher, through her explanations and reassurance, soon dispelled these fears. If they had continued it would have indicated that therapeutic treatment was needed.

When a child cries a teacher is always understanding. She will not show her concern and anxiety too obviously, nor fuss unnecessarily, but always be kind, reassuring and ready to give her sympathy and help.

In summarizing this chapter, we point out again that, while it is obviously necessary for a young child to accept help from his adults, the important thing is the child's attitude towards accepting this help. As an adult helps a child, it is through her own attitude and method of giving help that the child will come to realize that working together with others is not only a necessary but also an efficient way of living and, moreover, that it can be enjoyed by young and old alike.

Helping a child is natural and right. Furthermore such help assures that his growth towards independence and responsibility will be the gradual process it should be.

6. Helping a child learn to take responsibility

At times we are confused about the meaning of the term "independence." Some people suppose that when a child does things that are different from what other children do he is showing independence. Actually, such behaviour may not indicate true independence at all. Genuine independence is the ability and willingness to make decisions and to accept the results of these. We may decide to conform to the usual or perhaps to do something different, but it is the fact that we are able to *make* a decision rather than what the decision is or what its outcome is that indicates our independence.

Decisions by adults. As every adult knows, it is not easy to make decisions and to accept the responsibility for them. Whether we are buying a hat or trying to decide what political party to vote for, most of us find making decisions rather difficult. Sometimes we hesitate because we do not know exactly what the result or the "consequence" of a decision will be. We put a great deal of effort into predicting, as well as we can, what will happen when we decide to do one thing or the other. For instance, we may decide to buy a

54

certain stock rather than another because, from what we have heard, it seems to be a sounder investment. We may choose a blue rather than a green hat because we predict that our friends will think we look nicer in it. But as we cannot be sure of the actual outcome of this decision, making it is difficult.

Of course, in situations where we do know what the results will be, making a decision is relatively simple. For instance, we know with certainty that adding vanilla to a cake will give a definite flavour, whereas adding almond extract will give a different one. Where results are dependable and we know which result we want, we quickly and easily decide.

One reason that unpredictability makes decisions difficult is that there are often many variable factors to be taken into account. Suppose a man would like to buy a new house. He wants to do this because he has heard that a factory may be built near by. However, he has also heard that his firm may be transferring him to another city. He is confronted with "ifs" and "buts." He may say to himself, "I would like to move if a factory is going to be built but if I am transferred to another city, it would be silly to have purchased a new house." He must, therefore, make a prediction on these two possibilities and then decide whether to buy the new house or not.

Another factor that makes it difficult for us to make decisions is that each of us has to realize that the consequences of our decisions may affect others. The head of an organization who decides that his staff will all stay overtime on a certain evening certainly makes a decision the results of which affect others. The person who decides that he will not bother getting to work on time will certainly affect, by his decision, colleagues who must then carry on without him. If our government decides to raise taxes it is the citizens who must deal with the consequences.

Not only are decisions often difficult for adults to make but many find it hard to accept the results of what they have decided. It is not easy to accept the consequences of our own decisions when they turn out to be less satisfactory than we expected. When this happens, we are apt to keep blaming ourselves for our poor decisions, to regret what we did and worry about it. Certainly we will regret a poor decision, especially if we have inconvenienced others through our mistake. However, we can only try to accept the consequences of it and then let the experience help us to choose more wisely in the future.

Sometimes, indeed, we don't like admitting, even to ourselves, that we made what turned out to be a poor decision because it makes us feel extremely inadequate. And so we have many ways to avoid accepting the fact that these consequences resulted from our own action. These ways of transferring the responsibility from ourselves to someone else or to some circumstance are called in Blatz's terms "deputy agents." If a person's stock goes down, he may lay the blame on his friend who advised him to buy it or, if a man buys a new house and shortly after he is moved out of town, he may say, 'Well, my firm should have let me know sooner."

All of us often blame others to escape accepting responsibility for our own decisions. When we do this, we do not profit from our mistake. But when we take the responsibility for the outcome of our decisions we learn how to make better decisions in the future. One of the best things we can do for children is to give them an opportunity to learn both how to make decisions and to take the responsibility for them.

Decisions by children. Making decisions, as has been shown, can be exceedingly complicated. Therefore, for children, this experience should be made as simple as possible. The worst thing possible would be to allow young children to "decide everything for themselves." It would be equally foolish to expect them to decide in matters where the outcome is too hard to predict, that is, matters in which they don't know at all what the consequence will be. Usually a young child should be expected to make decisions only where the consequences are fairly obvious and also follow as consistently as possible. Then he will become aware of what happens when he makes a certain decision and this will help him in his future choice of behaviour.

In the beginning, with a very young child, the adult controls nearly all his behaviour so that he does not have to decide what he will or will not do. She removes hazardous objects and he will therefore not have to decide whether to play with them or not. She keeps him from behaviour that leads to unsatisfactory consequences for himself or others. One lecturer was asked, for example, "What do you do when a two-year-old pulls your hair?" A child's arms are perhaps fourteen inches long and so he answered. "You hold the child sixteen inches away from your head."

Soon, however, a child is ready to learn to make simple decisions and to discover their consequences. As we have said, a good way of ensuring that he gets this experience is to allow him to make his own choice, when possible, and then to see that some consistent consequence follows. Thus, the child will start to share with adults the responsibility for his behaviour. Two principles can be established: first, to limit the range within which a child makes decisions to matters which he is able to deal with and second, to make sure that we arrange the consequences of his decisions so that they are simple enough for him to understand.

II. ARRANGING LIMITS WITHIN WHICH A CHILD
CAN MAKE DECISIONS

Choice. Giving a child the right to choose for himself is a gradual process and does not mean that he is constantly being presented with a choice. The tendency has been to give too many choices to young children. This only confuses them and often causes them to become anxious or to worry and perhaps to develop the habit of arguing.

Sometimes adults are perplexed as to what kind of choice they should give to children. Choices can be offered when the child's decision will make little difference: "Would you like to play with a tricycle or a kiddy car?" or "Would you like a piece of bread or a biscuit?" (when both are offered).

But an adult will often say to a child, "Would you like to do thus and so?" when actually the child should not be permitted to make the decision. At the end of a day, when the child is called for, the teacher might say, "Would you like to go home now?" instead of saying, "It's time to go home now," or at home his mother might say "Would you like to go to bed now?" In both cases, the adult should make the decision.

Of course, it is not sensible to give a child a choice when the consequence might be harmful or dangerous. A child may not choose whether he will climb too high on a ladder or whether he will play on the road or on the sidewalk; a child may not choose to eat something that will make him sick or cut a piece of bread with a sharp knife.

A child's capacity. Before giving a child the opportunity to choose, an adult must be sure he will be *able* to carry it out. For instance, it would be silly to tell a child that, if he wants to, he can play outdoors, provided he comes home again in half an hour! He will not know when the half hour is up. It would also be foolish to let him choose to water a plant which is on too high a table for him to reach. He would probably pull it down on the floor! He should not be allowed to choose to hold open a door that is too heavy for him. It might swing back on someone else.

A child will be helped to start to take responsibility if he is offered a choice when he *can* decide for himself and can safely experience the outcome. Thus he begins to learn to accept the consequences of his decisions. This is the kind of choice that we are concerned with in our plan of learning.

Opportunities to choose. At the nursery school age, there are many of these opportunities. As we have mentioned before, a child is made aware of certain requirements and, when he understands them and is able to carry them out, he can be given opportunities to choose whether or not he will fulfil these requirements and to take the consequences of his decision. If he refuses to put on his snow boots before he goes out to play, he experiences the consequences of staying inside; and when he chooses to put his snow boots on, he experiences the consequences of going out. Here the teacher is really giving the child an opportunity to discover for himself why it is important to accept what he is required to do, whether he wants to do it or not! In this way we are helping the child to realize that requirements are a regular and necessary part of his life and that he will be happier if he accepts them.

A child's awareness. We also want a child to become aware that he is accepting these requirements because he, himself, chooses to do so rather than because an adult tells him to do so. A four-year-old child once refused to put on his snow boots before going out to play on a snowy morning. "I don't want to," he said. "All right," said the teacher, "But then you aren't ready to go out yet." Teacher and child waited at the door for a little while and the teacher busied herself with other matters. "Don't keep me waiting here," the child said in a few minutes. "*I'm* not keeping you here," answered the teacher. "You are keeping yourself here!" The child put on his boots with dispatch and went on his way.

III. SATISFACTORY AND UNSATISFACTORY CONSEQUENCES

If a child chooses to accept a requirement, the consequence will prove satisfactory to him. He will soon realize that this acceptance is worthwhile and this satisfactory consequence will be an incentive to accepting rather than refusing.

Rewards. Actually, one might say that this amounts to a reward. It is said that rewards are not the best way to help a child learn, but surely what we *mean* by rewards is the point to be considered. Really, everyone is rewarded for anything worthwhile he does, even if all he receives is a feeling of personal satisfaction. If a child accepts the requirements of playing with other children, not hitting them or taking their toys, he has the satisfaction of being able to stay with the others and enjoy himself. If he accepts the requirement of sitting down at a table when he wants to use the scissors he has the satisfaction of being able to cut and sew. However, some people use rewards as a bribe rather than as a logical and satisfactory outcome. A nursery school teacher must avoid saying, "If you do thus and so, I will give you a present," or "I will take you on our trip to the zoo." Because of this confusion as to meaning, we prefer to use the term "satisfactory consequence" rather than the word "reward."

Punishment. Conversely, when a child chooses to refuse a requirement, he discovers that an unsatisfactory consequence follows and, perhaps, this will help him to choose differently the next time. A nursery school teacher is often asked, "But doesn't this amount to a punishment and we thought you didn't believe in punishment?"

The word "punishment" can very well be left out of our plan of learning altogether. Punishment by an adult carries the implication of revenge and personal resentment. When a child is punished he may come to resent the adult's power and control instead of trusting it. Furthermore, the usual types of punishment often create fear and bewilderment in a child. Actually, punishment, instead of helping him learn to *take* responsibility, tends to make him avoid it, and he may very well begin to use what we have called "deputy agents." The kinds of unsatisfactory consequences that we are describing are very different from this. They are simple and obvious outcomes of a child's behaviour arranged to help him learn and not to frighten him.

Of course, many adults have stopped using punishment but have not taken the trouble to substitute another and better plan of helping a child learn. This leaves an adult in difficulties and the child out of control. Using the plan we describe takes time and trouble but it is worthwhile because it starts a child taking the responsibility for his own behaviour which is, after all, our ultimate goal for him. Furthermore, it is helping him to discover that a satisfactory consequence as well as an unsatisfactory one is the result of his own choice.

IV. NATURAL AND ARRANGED CONSEQUENCES

If a child were to put his finger in a fire, the consequence of being burned would teach him very quickly. This is a natural consequence, but it is one that obviously cannot be allowed to happen. There are, however, some natural consequences that a teacher *can* allow the child to experience: if he drops a big block on his toe, he will quickly learn that this will hurt; if he tries to eat the soap, he learns that it does not taste nice. But, at this age, a teacher usually has to arrange consequences which are not dangerous to a child.

Characteristics. Because a natural consequence teaches a child quickly and surely, a teacher will plan to have arranged consequences as much like natural ones as possible. This means that they should be obviously *reasonable* and *logical* and *relevant* to the situation. If a child refuses to put on his coat, he is not prepared to play outside with the other children. He plays inside as a consequence. If he deliberately tears a book, he is not permitted to have the book. If he throws his food on the floor, no more food is provided.

It is much better if the consequence can follow a child's behaviour *immediately*. If it is postponed until the next day, or even for an hour, it is apt to lose its meaning for a very young child. A teacher who says, "If you do thus and so, you won't be able to have a story tomorrow," is creating a poor kind of arranged consequence.

As a child grows older, he can remember circumstances for a longer time but, if a consequence is postponed at all, the teacher will have to remind the child of what led up to it. It is much more satisfactory to arrange for a consequence to follow immediately.

As we have said, if a consequence can be *consistently* the same and consistently follow a child's choice of behaviour, he will learn more quickly. On the other hand, if consequences are not consistent, it is more difficult for him to learn what we want him to learn. Suppose a child refuses to wash his hands before dinner. On Monday, his teacher sees that he accepts eating alone. On Tuesday, he again refuses to wash. The teacher is busy and "lets it go." Obviously, on Wednesday, the child will not know whether he has to wash his hands or not and may well refuse again in order to find out!

Variation of consequence. Although a teacher should arrange consequences so that, in general, they are consistent, she should remember that with different children the degree to which the consequence is used should vary according to their different attitudes and personalities. For instance, one child will learn from playing alone for a *very* short time while another child may have to play alone a longer time before he understands. One child will take the consequences of playing alone "in his stride," and not be upset at all, whereas another child might be unduly upset or frightened. For a child who is easily upset, playing alone just to one side of the playroom or playground would be the best consequence to arrange.

V. REMOVAL USED AS A CONSEQUENCE

Removal is one obvious kind of consequence that can be arranged. When a child has decided to behave in an inappropriate way, he can be removed from the person, things or activities that are giving rise to this behaviour. Usually this consequence is logical and relevant and can be carried out immediately and consistently.

Over-use. But some teachers use removal much too freely and some use it much too soon. They should stop to think whether being removed will be meaningful to a child. Often a teacher will remove a child from a group without considering *why* he is behaving the way he is.

In his routines, it might be that he has had too much done for him, or, on the other hand, it might be that he has been expected to do too much for himself. He has, therefore, become negative and resistant. Instead of removing him because of inappropriate behaviour, the teacher, by helping him and showing him, can help him to discover that accepting requirements is something that can be enjoyed and be worthwhile to him.

In play, it may be that the child does not yet know how to use his equipment or join with other children. In this case, what can he learn by being removed to play alone? It would be better, surely, for a teacher to help him learn how to play. She should even join in his activity and show him what he can do with his play material. Therefore, it is important that a teacher realize that a child should not be removed from things or people too soon. If he is to learn he must first *know* what is expected of him and *be able* to do it. Once he has learned some skills in his play and can understand the requirements asked of him, to be removed from the group *can* be a useful consequence.

In play. Let us imagine a child playing with blocks. His teacher notices that he is about to throw the blocks at another child. The simplest way to start teaching him would be to lay a restraining hand on his arm with a word of caution—"Be careful how you play with blocks" or "Remember to keep the blocks on the floor"—and add, "Let me show you what you can build with them."

Time passes and the child is growing and is able to understand. But he is still not accepting the rule of playing with blocks without throwing them. Yet, he is not at the stage where being removed from the playroom is the most useful consequence; so the teacher might take the blocks away and say, "You cannot have the blocks if you play with them that way, you know." Or she might say, "Move over here away from the other children and watch how *they* are playing and then you can try again."

More time passes and still this child has not learned. At this stage, giving him an opportunity to discover that his behaviour will bring unsatisfactory results will help him to learn. The teacher might say, "You don't seem to be able to remember about the blocks. If that's the way you want to play, you will have to play away from the other children for awhile." And, of course, the teacher must see that the child does this.

In a routine. Let us take another imaginary example. A child is told that it is time to get washed. This requirement is necessary and one that the child will have to accept if he is to fit into group living. The child refuses to come. If he is absorbed in some play project, the teacher should have chosen some other child first. However, soon he may be the last child, it is nearly dinnertime, and he still refuses. If he is a two-year-old, he probably does not understand what the teacher is talking about. In this case the teacher might lift the child in her arms, carry him into the washroom, show him the soap and the basin and say, "Here we go—you do your hands and I'll get the towel and we'll be ready for *dinner* in a jiffy."

If he is a little older, the teacher can remind him of the situation by saying, "Aren't you going to have dinner with us? Come along and I'll help you get ready."

If he is much older, however, and quite aware of both the incentive of having his dinner with the other children and the consequence of having it alone if he refuses to wash, the teacher can give him the responsibility of choosing whether he will get washed or not by saying, "All right, but do you remember you will have to have your dinner alone?" Then, if the child continues to refuse, she must see that he does have his dinner alone.

In a social situation. Let us take still another example of helping a child learn by accepting the consequences. A child starts to hit another child. The teacher will first wait a minute to see if the two children can settle this argument without her help. Perhaps the child was merely standing up for his own rights or protecting himself. Usually, however, the teacher will have to help the child learn that there are other ways of settling an argument. If the child is very young, she will restrain him with a word or two of explanation. If he is a little older, she might say something like "What's the trouble? If you want to play with the other children, you must try to keep from hitting them. These are his blocks too, remember." If, however, the child understands perfectly that the requirement for playing with other children is playing without hitting them, she might say, "If that's the way you want to play, you will have to come over here and play by yourself for awhile."

A child should always have some toy or book to play with when he is asked to play by himself. Furthermore, the period of time should not be too long, especially with a young child who may forget why he is there. Incidentally, the teacher, not the child, will decide the length of this period.

Behaviour to be ignored. Sometimes a child will refuse to accept a requirement or will behave in a certain way just to "tease" the teacher and to gain her attention. He enjoys the fuss that he can so easily create. If his behaviour will not cause any harm to anyone, obviously the most sensible consequence the teacher could arrange would be for her to pay no attention and do nothing at all. John, age three, is playing with a jigsaw puzzle. Suddenly he runs to the teacher and says "Look what I've done. I've put the puzzle in the wastepaper basket!" The teacher wisely says merely "Oh," and pays no more attention.

Adults are too inclined to look upon natural childish behaviour as a *problem* and thus make far too great an issue of it. A nursery school teacher must remember that children are in the process of learning and that when a child does not behave as she hopes, it is a natural part of his growing and not a problem at all. She must not make mountains out of natural little molehills, and the less fussing or worrying she does, the better. Usually the behaviour she is concerned about will just disappear.

Patience. Patterns of behaviour are formed slowly and an adult must be patient in looking for results. Of course, proverbially, patience is a virtue, but it all too often is used as an alibi for not taking the trouble to help a child learn. If a child's interest leads him to cutting up curtains, he will not learn much if his mother or teacher just patiently thinks, "Oh well, it is just a stage and he'll grow out of it." It really is a stage, but he may grow *into* it instead of *out* of it and innumerable curtains may disappear. Through an adult's help, he can discover that cutting paper can give him just as much pleasure. And, through a plan of learning by accepting the consequences of his behaviour, he will soon discover that, if he wants to cut, he must use paper or material provided for that purpose or accept the consequences of not being permitted to use scissors at all.

VI. ACCEPTING THE CONSEQUENCE

Protest. When a child is faced with the consequence of playing alone he may say, "I don't care. I wanted to play alone anyway!" His teacher will merely say, "Well that's all right, but whether you wanted to play alone or not, this is what you will have to do." Usually this is only an angry protest or perhaps an attempt to test the teacher's decision. The teacher, therefore, should pay no attention. However, once in a while, a child really *does* want to be by himself, and, as we have mentioned several times already, there should always be opportunities in a play period for a child to play by himself, if he wants to.

Crying. Perhaps a child will start to cry. If the teacher has made sure that the consequence of what he is doing will not be frightening to him, this crying will mean that he is not fearful but angry. One way to handle this situation is to lead or, if he slumps to the floor, carry him away from the other children to a place where he won't disturb their activities and also where he won't get as much attention. Sometimes it is not possible for a teacher to stay with him. But if she can stay with him, it seems to help him stop crying and control himself.

The teacher stays near him and, without getting excited or angry herself, "just waits" until the crying subsides. As always, she understands that this behaviour is natural with some children and that they need her *help*, not her disapproval or anger. However, one of a teacher's most important responsibilities is to help a child gradually learn to control himself and accept consequences without being unduly upset by them. So, without appearing over-concerned or giving too much attention, a teacher *will* try to help a child stop crying. Diversion may help with a very young child but an older child often becomes more angry if a teacher tries to placate and divert or coax and persuade him. It is probably better just to wait. Sometimes it helps a child to be held in a teacher's arms or on her lap.

However, while a teacher is waiting with a child, she can tell him to "try to stop crying" so that they can talk about it. There is no use trying to explain anything to a crying child because he doesn't hear. Usually, if a child realizes that a teacher is there to help and not to scold him, he will stop crying in a minute or two. When he feels better the teacher can explain what his trouble is all about. The child will have to accept the consequence of playing alone as he was told in the first place, but in a little while, the teacher can go with him and help him choose a form of behaviour that results in his being with the other children again. Occasionally, a child may feel ashamed of crying and try too hard to stop. In this case, a teacher can help him realize that, if he wants to cry; that's all right too, and nothing to be ashamed of.

Very, very occasionally a child will become so intensely angry that he doesn't know what he is doing. In this case, a teacher should stay with him to protect him from harm. Sometimes a child who is very upset will become even more so if he is left alone. Needless to say, a teacher shows no personal irritation if a child behaves angrily towards her.

It is important to help a child learn that he never gains his ends by this angry crying. A teacher must outlast a child's protest. He soon comes to realize that it is rather futile and it is not long before this kind of crying disappears altogether.

Crying such as we have described is exceptional. As we have said before, it is surprising that there is so little in a nursery school. If a child did cry a lot, it would probably be an indication that he needed extra help and reassurance from the teacher in all his activities. The teacher would review his behaviour as a whole, both at home and at school, and, with the help of more expert advice, plan a special programme for him.

Sulking. Sometimes, when a child must accept the consequence of his behaviour, he will not cry, but sulk. Obviously he is hoping to gain someone's sympathy or attention. It is better if a teacher does not criticize or scold but ignores this behaviour altogether. A little later, when the child feels better, she can re-interest him in some play activity as though nothing had happened at all.

A teacher's attitude. As in every part of our plan of guiding a child's learning, it is his teacher's attitude that is the most important factor. In helping a child learn by accepting the consequences, his teacher will, as we have seen, give him the right to choose for himself, provided he is old enough to understand what this will involve. In other words, his conduct is "up to him." But this does *not* mean that the teacher is impersonal, cold or not interested. Her affection for the child, her interest in him, is personal, warm, deep and unchanging. If a child has confidence and trust in his teacher, he will not be afraid to say "no" to a requirement. He will know that, even though his teacher will make sure that a consequence follows his refusal, he will not lose her support. In fact, interestingly enough, her consistency of control will increase his trust in her.

Disapproval. A teacher should not have any personal resentment towards a child when he does not come up to her expectations. There must never be a "pitched battle" between adult and child. Of course, it would be unnatural if an adult were not to show disapproval in some situations—for instance, when the child was found cutting up the curtains! But disapproval should be of the behaviour and not of the child. After all, if a child behaves like this, it may well be an adult's fault in the first place!

It is easy for an adult to become irritated and cross, which usually adds confusion to the situation. A teacher should not become excited and emotional but try to be matter-of-fact and remember that her job is to help the children. She is always a teacher and a friend. Moreover, a teacher should avoid criticism, scolding, moralizing and post mortems, because these immediately make a child think that the teacher feels a personal resentment towards him: the less talk the better. What she is trying to do is to make the child realize that she is "on his side" to help him with his difficulty.

As she guides the children through the day, a teacher's attitude should be one of expecting the best; she will then probably get it. But, even if she doesn't, it is not catastrophic: life will go on in a nursery school. It is the children who make it such a wonderfully thrilling place. It would be odd indeed if they always did what they were expected to do. Furthermore, they would not be discovering that, like everyone else, they too have a right to be different.

VII. A NURSERY SCHOOL TEACHER'S RESPONSIBILITY

The nursery school teacher has a complicated job. At one and the same time she is giving children an opportunity to grow in *dependence* and an opportunity to grow in *independence*. As she teaches them to accept requirements (chapter 4) and as she teaches them to accept help (chapter 5), she is fostering their dependence. As she encourages their self-effort (chapter 3) and their taking of responsibility (chapter 6), she is furthering their independence.

A teacher will discover that each child is different in his pattern of developing dependence and independence. At the nursery school age, some children are ready for a good deal of opportunity to take responsibility while others are hardly ready to begin. For some of these children their most important need is to learn to accept dependence. The proportion of emphasis a teacher puts on these two aspects of a child's growth will be determined by his age of readiness. Her ability to make a judgement on this score will increase only as she comes to know and understand each child with whom she is working.

Learning to be dependent on adults and to be independent on one's own are the beginnings of growing up: they are the important things to be established during infancy and the pre-school years. However, another aspect of development begins to appear during this period. That is, through the child's relationships with his contemporaries, he experiences a new kind of dependency which we have called mature dependency. Very little of this really appears before a child is five years old, but the roots of it begin to grow as a reciprocal reliance on his contemporaries develops. As a child grows older, relationships of both an intimate nature and a more casual kind emerge. Gradually, a child grows into a person who functions independently amid interdependent relationships. These terms a nursery school teacher need not consider too deeply, but she should be aware that what she is doing lays the foundation for the essentials of mental health in adulthood.

7.   A nursery school teacher's day

A nursery school teacher may often be exhausted, but she will never be bored. As day follows day, she finds herself engrossed in countless matters of absorbing interest.

Atmosphere. One of her greatest ambitions is to create for the children in her school a certain "atmosphere." It is almost impossible to describe in words what is meant by this term. Of first importance, of course, is the achievement of a day that runs smoothly and with a minimum of confusion. This creates a sense of ease in which rushing and fussing, worrying and uncertainty, have little place. The feeling of ease also comes from the children's realizing that all is well in the school because the teachers are there to "look after things" and that they can relax and feel safe in their care. But there should also be a feeling of exhilaration. This comes through the children's knowledge of all the wonderful things there are to do in a nursery school, and their finding out the fun of companionship with their friends and with their teachers too.

Since endless planning is needed in order to create this ideal atmosphere, it is essential that the whole nursery school staff share this ambition and work together as a team to achieve it.

Timetable. Some schools like to function with a plan but without a timetable. However, a daily timetable can be of help to the staff.

There are various ways of arranging it: some schools prefer a staff member to be in charge of the younger or older children for a week, month, or even longer; other schools find it better to change a teacher's responsibilities daily. The value of this latter plan is that each teacher comes to know every child in the school and each child comes to know every teacher. Furthermore, each teacher becomes familiar with every situation in the school and will, therefore, be ready to assume responsibility in any part of it. The supervisor can prepare this timetable once a week, but every morning she will have to check it and make any necessary changes.

In the preceding chapters, we have said that a fairly regular daily programme is of help to the children. It is also a help to the teachers if they can know what happens next. Of course, the programme will differ in different setups. A nursery school programme probably includes: nurse's inspection as the children arrive, outdoor active play, cloakroom, toilet, indoor play; special group activities such as music, story, carpentry, clay; short relaxation, dinner, toilet, and rest. In a school where the children stay late, outdoor and indoor playtimes, special activities and tea will be added.

It is important for the supervisor to arrange the timetable so that each member of her staff may have some time for relaxation during the day and, when it is possible, a cup of coffee in the morning is a good thing too. The time for this coffee break is sometimes so short that it could be called a "coffee crack." Naturally no teacher allows a break to interfere with her responsibilities. On the contrary, each teacher will take her responsibilities very seriously indeed, realizing that her promptness, punctuality and sense of responsibility are absolutely necessary to a smoothly running school.

A nursery school teacher's main interest is, of course, the children themselves. All nursery school teachers should feel that working with pre-school children is one of the most rewarding and thrilling experiences there is. Year after year, children will continue to be of endless fascination to a teacher. Their joys and their sorrows become, in part, her own.

Her interest, however, does not stop at her enjoyment of the children; she is vitally concerned with the development of each individual child in her school. Her daily contacts with the children help her to become aware of how each child is developing. Of course, impressions are often unreliable, and so these daily contacts need to be supplemented.

Records. Keeping a written record of a child's behaviour is the only sure way of knowing how he is developing. Most schools hold a weekly staff meeting and at that time these records can be reviewed. They will prove of invaluable assistance if it is considered necessary to decide on a special plan for helping a child. Even a small nursery school staff will find it possible to keep records if there is a well-organized plan for handling them. The record form should be set up so that it can be understood clearly and is easy to use; it should, of course, be stored near at hand. All that is needed on the record is a simple statement of what a child does in certain situations and what his teacher does about it. Interpretation of the behaviour can be done later.

Records are of such value to a teacher that they more than make up for the trouble of keeping them. Obviously, these records will be of great help when the teacher discusses a child with his parents.

Parents. A nursery school teacher has a great responsibility to the parents of her children. The parents must be encouraged to feel free to discuss their children at any time with the teacher. It will be mutual help to teacher and parent if they can discuss together how a child is getting along at school and how he is getting along at home. A teacher must make parents realize that the school is ,in no way attempting to be a substitute for the home, but rather to be a supplement to it.

Some parents will need to be reassured that there is no cause to worry about minor matters; others may need help in planning for their children. A nursery school teacher will, of course, recognize her limitations in discussing a child with his parents and, if necessary, she will be ready to refer them to someone more qualified than herself. A teacher can be of help to parents but parents can also be of great help to a teacher. Therefore, as a teacher plans for each child while he is at school, she will seek the information only parents can give and be guided by their judgement.

In many schools, it is most convenient for a teacher to see parents when they bring their children in the morning. If such a time cannot be arranged, the teacher must make an appointment at the parents' convenience.

Every day a teacher should take time to inform parents of anything unusual that has happened to their children: if one has been exposed to measles; if he fell and scratched his knee; or if he did not feel hungry at dinner time. If a parent does not call for a child, the teacher will telephone any message of importance. On the other hand, parents should feel free to call the teacher and tell her anything out of the ordinary that they would like her to do.

A teacher should also arrange for parents to observe in the school if they wish. Most parents are enthusiastic about this and say that it is of the greatest help to them as they plan their children's programme at home. These "parent visiting days" can be one of the greatest pleasures for both parents and teacher. The teacher is proud, the parents are proud and, of course, the children love it!

Most parents will appreciate and be interested in attending a few evening meetings throughout the year. Here they can learn not only what goes on in the nursery school but also why the teacher has arranged the programme in a certain way. The teachers can plan these groups to meet the interests of their parents.

All these contacts with the parents will help both teacher and parents to feel that they are working together in their mutual interest—the child.

Emergencies. No matter how carefully a nursery school teacher plans a day, emergencies occasionally occur. A teacher must keep her head. She must not become flustered and excited, as this will upset the children. By her desk there will be a telephone list for the fire department, the police, the school doctor, the hospital, an ambulance, a taxi company. There will also be a list of children's names, addresses and telephone numbers. A completely equipped first aid tray should always be available in the school. If a teacher decides that a child is ill, she will call the child's mother and doctor for directions. If this is not possible, she will call the school doctor. She will be guided by the rules and regulations of the local Departments of Health and Welfare and act accordingly.

Not all emergencies are serious, of course. The water or electricity may be turned off; the fire bell may ring for fire drill. The important thing is that a nursery school teacher must handle all emergencies in such a way that the children will not become anxious or frightened. She must make her decisions quickly and then, quite calmly and in her most matter-of-fact way, direct the children in any necessary change of procedure.

Visitors. Visits to a school will be arranged for parents, but there will be other visitors who will want to come. If a school is equipped with observation screens, it is a simple matter to accommodate visitors. But even when there are no screeens, it is interesting to note that, if a school has a regular programme which goes ahead without change, the children will pay surprisingly little attention to visitors. However, the number of visitors in any school should be controlled. To have too many strangers in the school too often becomes disturbing to both children and staff. Visitors can be asked to inquire ahead of time when they may come and the teacher can arrange certain days for them. She must make them feel welcome and the exchanging of ideas and experiences will prove stimulating to them both.

Student training. In some schools, a programme of student training is added to a teacher's responsibilities. This becomes an interest second only to a teacher's interest in her children and infinite hours go into planning a student's programme.

When a student first comes into the school, she feels bewildered and confused. A day or two for observations in the school will be of help to her. But one of the best ways for a student to increase her knowledge of children, and to realize how much she has to learn, is to start her practice immediately. Of course, she may become discouraged if she is given too much responsibility all at once. A good way to help a student gain self-confidence is to give her some responsibility in situations where she feels most comfortable. For instance, what to do in a cloakroom or washroom is clearly defined for a student. Therefore, at first, she may feel more confident in these routines than in the playrooms. Some students find it easy to tell a story to the children, whereas others may want to wait until they have more confidence and skill. It is easy to handle a single child and soon a student can be given responsibility with a small group of children, but it will take a little time and experience before a student has learned the skill necessary for handling a large group of nursery school children by herself. On the other hand, some students want more responsibility than the teacher arranges for them. Perhaps they do not realize that handling children is not quite as easy as it looks! They should understand that, of necessity, for the care of the children and for the running of the school, responsibility can be given only as they become more experienced.

The children sometimes "try out" new students. They are almost certain to meet situations of difficulty which the staff do not meet. A staff member may have to step in and give extra help. It is a good plan to tell a student that such situations may occur and that if they do she need not feel inadequate.

A new student will find it helpful to have a more experienced staff member with her to demonstrate the school procedures and show her how to carry them out. A school which has a student training programme should also have a large enough staff to make this arrangement possible.

It is important that a student understand that the necessary direction she will receive is never meant as personal criticism. A teacher's directions are given as information and not as criticism. However, when this information is given to a student, there are a few points that a more experienced teacher should keep in mind. When a student needs direction, it is usually because she does not *know* what is expected of her. Direction should be given at a suitable time, preferably ahead of the occasion for which it is needed, and not in front of the children or other members of staff. It should be given only when necessary and in such a way that it can be easily understood. Direction is meant to *help* a student and care must be taken not to give it in a way that may hurt feelings or cause resentment or a feeling of inferiority.

It will be of help to a student if a weekly seminar is arranged to discuss her observations and practice. In these seminars, the general principles of the school procedures can be explained and ways of carrying them out discussed. However, this information should be given gradually too. If too much is given all at once, a student may become self-conscious and unsure of herself.

A teacher should realize that in a group of students there will be many differences in personalities and she will also remember that there are various ways of carrying out the principles of nursery school procedures. When a student becomes skilled in her practice, she will, more or less, develop her own techniques but, in the beginning, she should learn to welcome information as a valuable factor in her gaining of experience.

It is a teacher's responsibility to make students feel that they are useful and valuable members of staff. The students, in their turn, can be useful only if they are willing to take their responsibilities seriously and carry them out to the best of their ability. Together, student and teacher can take a pride in the running of the school and, together, they can enjoy the thrill of working with the children.

Highlights of the day. Most nursery school teachers have some special interest which they can share with the children, such as music, stories, dancing, dramatics or any of the creative arts. Since no programme should try to provide them all, certain ones can be selected for special emphasis.

A highlight of a teacher's day is the time set aside for story telling or music. Of course, throughout the day, the children will often look at books, have a story or sing songs, but a special time, as well, can be planned.

Discovering what kind of story will interest children most and acquiring the art of story telling are among the most worthwhile and rewarding things a teacher can do; she will face a rapt audience whether she tells a story to two or three children or to a group of twenty.

In the same way, music groups can be a thrilling experience for both teacher and children. Here is the one place in the school day where they are participating together in a mutual interest and enjoyment. A teacher need not feel diffident about leading a group of children in music. For this age, it is not as important that a teacher be a skilled musician as that she have an understanding of children and of what will interest them most. It is through her enthusiasm and ingenuity that the children's interest in music is developed. A child may always choose whether or not he wants to join a music group, but it is up to his teacher to make it so interesting and so much fun that he will indeed want to join. Her aim is to arrange a musical experience in which children will come to realize that music belongs to everyone and is something that *everyone* can enjoy. Not only do most children love to come to the music time but often it will be found that all the teachers in the school are there too! Vistors, parents, all can join in the singsong if they wish. It is indeed the highlight of the day.

A nursery school teacher's day is filled with many matters: children, parents, students, visitors, timetables, records, emergencies. And after the children have gone home, there is the school to tidy for the next day, play materials to be replenished, dolls to be washed, repairs to be made, records to be filed, letters to answer, messages to parents, lectures to be given, meetings to attend, reports for governing bodies—and tomorrow is another day! Being a nursery school teacher is indeed a full-time job.

EPILOGUE

Preschool teaching—
An historical perspective

Dorothy A. Millichamp

Pre-school education in Canada and the United States always has been associated with child study so that the innovations and changes which have taken place in nursery school teaching follow the succession of research discoveries in early child development. As different aspects of the young child's development have become the focus of investigation the teacher has been called upon to shift her teaching goals and readjust her programme to serve yet another child need. This tie with child study has been the strength of pre-school education. It has kept the child at the centre of the programme. The difficulty for the teacher has been to so integrate each new developmental value into her teaching that other aspects of the child's development also continue to be served. What follows in this epilogue is an attempt to put the changing goals of pre-school teaching into perspective.

In the 1950's when this book was written, the attention of investigators was focussed on early personality development and particularly on the development of interpersonal relations between child and adult during the first years of life. It was the time when the mental health of infants and young children was at the forefront of enquiry. For the pre-school teacher of the fifties the heightened emphasis on child-adult relations called for a revision of her role as teacher and a new emphasis on child-teacher interaction. Of course thoughtfully planned communication by teachers to children had been a part of pre-school teaching from the beginning but in the early days the interpersonal aspects of living with children were simply taken for granted.

I. THE EARLY TEACHING GOALS

The early nursery schools of the twenties were set up to observe the behaviour of young children directly in a natural environment and teachers were members of the research team. At this time the investigators were convinced that important psychological growth is occurring in the pre-school years. Particular significance was attached to the young child's spontaneous play activity as a source of both physical and psychological growth and not merely a childish pastime. So, these early nursery schools were designed to provide the young child with appropriate opportunities and the freedom to carry out his own experimental activities.

Such a goal necessitated a special approach to teaching and a new kind of school teacher, as Harriet Johnson described in 1928. The pre-school teacher was expected to support the child's initiative and self-effort; to encourage self-help and self-direction which the child could manage; to offer opportunities for spontaneous learning and creative effort in physical, sensory and mental activities. It was her responsibility to control the children as necessary but without repressive or punitive threats and with acceptance of the young child's immaturity. On the whole it was a watchful, helpful, background role in a carefully planned setting with a minimum of direct teaching.

Looking back, this approach obviously did much to build healthy child-adult relations even though this was not a main purpose. Certainly there was a mutual exchange of respect between the child and teacher to enhance the child's sense of worth both to others and in his own eyes. The child was assured of the teacher's interest and support on his behalf and of her help to fulfil his needs and wants. The message from his nursery school adults was positive and consistent.

II. NEW TEACHING GOALS ARE INTRODUCED

As study proceeded within the nursery school, new knowledge led to new developmental goals in pre-school education. Gesell led the way in charting the "ages and stages" of early behaviour and this information provided teachers with a more precise guide as to what they might expect of young children and how to plan for them. The personal routines of the nursery school day were considered important for a child's feeling of satisfaction and his beginning sense of responsibility. Research observation of social interaction among pre-schoolers became possible. It was a surprise at the time to discover that a child's sociability comes about in step-by-step fashion and is a matter of exploratory learning and problem solving. These findings had considerable impact on nursery school programming. Greater emphasis was placed on social activity and the relative importance of individual versus social learning was debated. In a number of nursery schools social learning was given priority. This innovation also brought about discussion of the amount and kind of control which the teacher should exercise. Here too, teachers began to differ in their approach.

By the 1940's a different influence was beginning to affect pre-school education. Findings from clinical work with young children brought new insights regarding child personality and individual differences to be found among young children. Of particular concern to teachers was evidence from clinicians that a young child may build up emotional distress, frustrations and fears of a pervasive nature without him giving them direct expression. Although they found it hard to accept at first, teachers gradually became understanding of the need for both positive and negative emotional expression in all young children, also, of their need for ready adult acceptance and help in dealing with their feelings. Thus another dimension was added to pre-school teaching, one which brought the teacher into closer contact with each child. This was the beginning of a shift of emphasis in nursery school values toward mental health.

III. MENTAL HEALTH BECOMES THE FOCUS

It was John Bowlby's striking statements on the adverse effects of maternal deprivation which brought the whole matter of relations between child and adult to the forefront of child care in the early 1950s. Child workers were shocked to find that a child can grow up lacking a basic sense of relationship with his human world. They were disturbed to realize that the ability to form interpersonal ties cannot be assumed, that this ability develops over time and is dependent on the experiences provided for a child particularly in his home. Bowlby gave a new significance to the infant period as the starting point of interpersonal involvement and to the pre-school period as a critical time when the child's affiliations are strengthening but still are subject to breakdown. While the theoretical aspects of his thesis were under debate professional workers already were questioning child care practices from this new point of view.

For practical purposes it became necessary to understand the normal course of interpersonal development and Erickson's psychoanalytical concept of healthy personality growth was widely accepted. In Canada Blatz's theory of "security" provided a guide for building up salutary child-adult interaction. Both propositions place responsibility on adult care and especially on maternal care in the early stages of development. Early in life the infant must have the opportunity to grow in dependence and to become, in Erickson's terms, "trusting", or as Blatz calls it, "dependently secure" through interaction with his human world. Both considered this first phase of development as prerequisite for the second, which is described as a sense of "autonomy" or "independent security", that is, the beginning of sustained outgoing effort and self realization. This second phase is expected to strengthen in the pre-school years provided adult support is forthcoming. At this time the child reaches a more mature phase of affiliation in which he gains confidence in himself as a person among people. These two features of personality were considered as the groundwork of mental health and provided new goals for the care of infants and young children.

As part of the general concern aroused by Bowlby's findings, nursery schools and day care came under criticism. Should a child be separated from his mother at this critical age or, as some claimed, is he ready to extend his relations outside the home? Procedures in the nursery school were scrutinized, and immediate results included a more careful judgment of each child's readiness to leave home and greater involvement of the parent within the school. In regard to teaching practices, it became evident that the role of the pre-school teacher met the stated needs of a pre-schooler for continuous support in his outgoing endeavours, that is, for the second phase of his development in interpersonal ties. What appeared to be missing was a consciously worked out plan to meet the child's dependent needs and to foster his reliance on and trust in adult care and concern.

Care and concern were a natural part of pre-school teachers' interaction with children. What they had to learn was to express these more directly and clearly. Personal attention to the child's routine needs, his emotional outbursts of pleasure and pain, his seemingly unreasonable demands for attention, the hellos and good-byes between child and adult, conversations, holding a hand or sitting on a knee, all these gained new meaning and became a part of teaching. Applying the principles of relationship it became easier for a teacher to understand the immature child as one who has not sufficient trust to embark on learning effort. She was able to recognize the pseudo-independent pre-schooler who appears so able but actually is afraid to express dependence. In short, mental health, both preventive and therapeutic, became an important aspect of pre-school teaching, and in many programmes the acquisition of abilities took second place.

IV. COGNITIVE LEARNING BECOMES THE FOCUS

By the 1960's child study had moved on and again pre-school education followed in its wake. This time cognitive development was the particular subject of enquiry. In fact, viewed historically, attention had come full circle back to study of the young child's motor, sensory, perceptual, conceptual and language development, but with a difference. The new emphasis was on the process of learning and on teaching. Piaget's theoretical view of the successive stages of cognitive development led the way. Guilford's work on the "structure of intelligence" made it possible to think of child intellect in qualitative instead of quantitive terms. Skinner's experimental studies of learning provided a new basis for teaching models and behaviour modification. Gradually, the idea emerged that during the first years of life the child is learning to be intelligent; that if his thinking processes are to change and mature this requires stimulation within a social milieu. Again, as in the case of child mental health, the adult role gained in importance as an essential ingredient of the developmental process.

For the first time pre-school teaching *per se* became an important subject of research, the question was, how should the child be taught in order that he progress intellectually? Current nursery school programmes were examined critically and new teaching procedures designed for experimental trial. These varied, some were built on Piaget's system and others involved direct instruction in intellectual skills. Differences of opinion arose concerning the relative merits of adult structured versus spontaneous play activity for cognitive learning. However, the child's need for teacher planning, stimulation and intervention to sustain progressive learning in this area was generally accepted.

The immediate outcome of the current discoveries underway was to give pre-school education a new public image. For the first time in its history it was viewed as a means of direct preparation for later schooling. The Head Start Programme introduced in the United States in 1964 reflected this new purpose. The argument was logical. If intellectual abilities are a matter of learning then it may be assumed that some of the deficits found among school age children originate in the pre-school period, especially where the young child's home environment has lacked intellectual stimulation. So, nursery schools for disadvantaged pre-school children became a specialized area of pre-school teaching. Insights into the qualitative differences among children in their intelligence also resulted in better understanding and new ways of working with young mentally retarded children and those with perceptual handicaps. These adaptions further diversified pre-school teaching.

For the pre-school teacher working amid the confusion of ideas for cognitive teaching, it was difficult. Not only had she an additional goal to incorporate and new knowledge and techniques to acquire, there was also the question of teaching priorities to be worked out. The values of pre-school education seemed to be at issue and teachers had many questions to raise. Is the child's personal-social progress and psychological well being less important than his intellectual and academic achievement? Is it necessary to hurry a child in the acquisition of letter and number skills? Is direct teaching compatible with the encouragement of initiative? Will interpersonal ties between child and adult be weakened by more teacher expectations and instruction? How should the choice of teaching goals be made in the best interests of the child? Such was the state of things at the beginning of the 1970's.

V. ASSEMBLING THE GOALS OF PRE-SCHOOL EDUCATION TODAY

It is not necessary to make a choice from among the teaching goals and the education procedures which have emerged in pre-school education. Today's pre-school teacher may opt for another course of action. She may choose to integrate all these goals within her teaching programme and to adapt any number of the available procedures to serve her purposes, or she may create her own. Perhaps this is the innovation and the challenge for the pre-school educator of the seventies. Pieced together, the long-term findings of child study become the guidelines for accomplishing this task. Now the young child can be thought of as developing on several major fronts at once which together lead toward his maturity. Because these components of development are interrelated, his progress in one is dependent upon progress in another; there is an order inherent in development as a whole as well as in its parts. Furthermore it has become evident that development does not happen to a child, it is the result of his own learning effort and for this he is in need of adults.

Looked at practically, it appears that the child in nursery school or day nursery needs adult help in three main areas of his learning: in the development of mental health strengths, in the acquisition of physical and cognitive facilities, and in the development of social relations with his peers. The teacher like the child will be working on these three fronts at the same time but her teaching emphasis and programme will vary according to the maturity of her group in each area.

Teaching for mental health. It has become apparent that young children need their mental health strengths, that is, interpersonal ties with adults and freedom from pervasive anxiety, in order to cope fully with the other tasks of learning. If an adult hopes to teach a child she must be sure that he is able to use her, to accept and seek her guidance. This requires a growing sense of trust on the child's part which leads to comfortable interaction between child and teacher. The child develops in relationship through experience, which includes cognitive learning by percept and concept as well as affective experiences. Therefore it remains for the teacher to decide what meaning she would like the child to give adults, at least those in his school world. In the give and take between teacher and child, a child gradually builds up proof that he can safely rely on his teachers and as he responds to their recurring personal support and finds this good, he learns to believe in their concern for him as a person. A child may react tentatively at first to the teachers' expectations and controls but if these are consistently carried out and are meaningful to him they help to build his sense of trust in his adult world. Children differ in the length of time they take to establish this relationship and each requires a somewhat different quality of interaction. A few young children already have acquired distrust of their adult world. Special therapeutic planning will be necessary for these children.

Many young children enter school with a good set of child-adult relations on which to build. For these children the teaching emphasis can be on other areas of learning. However, disadvantaged and otherwise handicapped children often will be in need of catch-up experience to increase their confidence in adults and in themselves. Children in day care, whatever their competency, must have continuing opportunity to depend as well as to be independent to make up for the experiences which they are missing at home. This will be particularly important for the very young pre-schoolers who now come to day nurseries.

So, the teacher's emphasis on mental health will vary with her group and will change as the children progress. Interpersonal relationship and the positive emotion which it engenders has been described as the ground work of development. It also may be thought of as the ground work of pre-school teaching. Miss Fletcher's plan of guidance outlined in this book suggests some practical ways of providing such a base.

Teaching for cognitive development. To teach with mental health in mind does not mean that the child's acquisition of abilities is less important, and in practice the two teaching jobs will proceed at once. Mental health consideration may determine to some extent the method of teaching which is employed. Nowadays there is a good deal of information available to teachers about the young child's motor, sensory, perceptual, conceptual and language development. Because of the interdependence of these facets of development as outlined by Piaget, they are usually considered as components of cognitive learning. Knowledge of the way in which the young child learns also is available, and a number of methods have been designed for programming cognitive learning. These vary in form of content, type of help and guidance, amount of direct instruction and in the importance given to free enterprise. In general these programmes supply the teacher with new and more sophisticated teaching skills by which to stimulate and direct the child's learning effort. A main question, still unresolved, is the balance necessary between direct and indirect teaching. This decision becomes easier to make if the child's total development is taken into account.

It is probable that until a child's sense of reliance and his willingness to put forth effort are well under way he will profit most from free choice activity with well selected play materials. This does not minimize the teacher's role. Unlike the free-play programme of the early days, it is now advised that the teacher be in the foreground ready to point out, to suggest, to explain and inform, to talk with the child, in all to enhance the child's awareness and carry him a step further in perception toward conceptual thinking. This procedure may be thought of as incidental teaching in which the child sets the pace and the teacher acts, in Burton White's terms, as his "consultant." It has the advantage that cognitive learning, reliance on the teacher and initiative can be encouraged at the same time and on an individual basis. Young pre-schoolers will need a good deal of this experience and it is certainly a safe beginning for disadvantaged children. Of course this procedure, as for all cognitive teaching, requires that teachers understand the way in which young children think. According to Piaget the structure of a child's concepts is not only simpler but is different from adults. Also to be taken into account are the different stages of cognitive structure. If teaching intervention is not appropriate to the child's present way of thought then it can become intrusion. Equally important is the teacher's judgment that a child is better left to his own devices.

Varying degrees of direct teaching can be combined with a basic free-activity programme. One-to-one sessions in which the adult sets the cognitive learning problem for the child are useful in several ways. They offer maximum opportunity for the teacher to adapt to the child's level of cognition and his facility for problem solving so that success can be part of his experience. Furthermore, the child learns not only how to work under direction but to enjoy it. Most disadvantaged children respond eagerly to these sessions because of the individual attention afforded. Because such children often lag not only in cognitive abilities but in the interest and curiosity necessary for learning, personal adult stimulation may be greatly needed. There is no doubt that day nursery children could profit in many ways from private adult teaching time. The problem for the teacher is to arrange this in a busy schedule. Fowler has suggested small group projects set up to teach a specific cognitive ability. This is a flexible approach allowing the teacher to plan catch-up learning projects for some children and advanced cognitive tasks for the most competent of her group. Using this procedure she still can be in touch with each child.

The method of direct instruction to larger groups introduced by Bereiter and Engleman obviously reduces the personal impact of the adult, although the group as a whole receives plenty of adult stimulation and praise. Under this system the children learn to respond to a sequence of very specific cognitive tasks designed to prepare them for later schooling. It is not easy to estimate the effect of this form of teaching on other aspects of the child's development. The method was designed primarily for disadvantaged children with cognitive deficiencies. Since these children also have other developmental lags it seems probable that exclusive use of this method is not enough. To progress in basic cognitive functions the child also must be moving ahead in related aspects of his development. Therefore disadvantaged children will need a broadly based programme and perhaps several teaching approaches for their cognitive learning are better than any one.

Of course, whole group teaching is not new to pre-school teachers. Most schools and day nurseries gather the children together at least once a day. The new ways of introducing cognitive learning are interesting for both the children and the teachers. As well as music and stories there are perceptual and conceptual activities and games. These can be used to increase the children's awareness and interest in the things and doings around them, that is, in materials and furnishings, in space and time sequences, in the day's activities, and in people at home and school. Hopefully what is done in these directed group sessions will carry over to the children's free activity. The teacher can do much to integrate these separate experiences for the children.

Day nursery staff have a unique opportunity for cognitive teaching as well as a special responsibility since time and energy are short at home. Starting with a basic free-choice play programme, a variety of teaching projects can be spaced throughout the day and the year, perhaps dovetailed to each teacher's specialty. The children can be involved as they are ready and programming advanced with their progress. All this can be co-ordinated with other goals. The necessary ingredient for the teacher is time to plan.

There is no doubt that in pre-school education cognitive learning and teaching are here to stay even though new findings in child study will introduce new goals in the future. Sufficient knowledge and practical guides now are available to make it possible for the teacher to put cognitive teaching in place as an integral part of pre-school education.

Teaching for academic readiness. Is it also the pre-school teacher's responsibility that young children learn their letters and numbers at nursery school? Opinions vary in this regard from the very positive to the very negative and research is still at the experimental stage. The teacher is wise to take a middle course. It is evident from recent school age investigations such as Mary Meeker's work in California that persistent academic difficulties often may be traced to specific deficits in basic intellectual operations. From such findings it may be deducted that a thorough preparation in cognitive activities, as already discussed, is the pre-school teacher's best guarantee that a young child will manage his future schooling. However, there is another aspect to this preparation for school which is engaging the attention of investigators.

Many children live from their earliest years in what might be called a literary home environment where the use of reading, writing and numbers is an obvious part of their adult world and of conversational exchange. As teachers provide a similar experience at nursery school these children become curious about symbols. As they develop intellectually interest grows and their minds reach out in an attempt to manipulate these adult sponsored devices for problem solving. They are becoming ready to explore the use of symbols. For some well developing children this readiness of interest as well as intellect happens during their pre-school years. In this case teachers have to be prepared to give the kind of guidance, within the play situation, which encourages experimental effort. Pedantic teaching could be discouraging to a child at this point.

On the other hand, there are children, particularly those from culturally disadvantaged homes, who do not have a natural introduction to cultural symbols nor the adult models to give them special value. Therefore at nursery school they will need repeated references to reading, writing and numbers done within the context of their daily activities and with sufficient teacher emphasis to intrigue the children: a child's own name written down, his house number by which to find him, his need for two shoes, books which tell him stories and so forth. These less developmentally advanced children may not reach the stage of cognition necessary to use symbols meaningfully for some time but if they are to be amenable to teaching by school age then reading, writing and arithmetic must have worthwhile meaning to them. Day nursery children inevitably will miss much of the casual but recurring literary stimulation gained at home so that here again the teacher has more to provide.

Some head start programmes have tried out direct group instruction with letter and number content. This method of teaching does bring about rote learning, but beyond this there are more questions raised than answers forthcoming. Nor have the effects of instructional programmes on television been thoroughly investigated.

However, young children are watching television and nowadays it behooves the teacher to be prepared for the pre-school television fan. He may come to school with letters and numbers on his mind often mixed in with fancy, fun and games. At least he has some beginning awareness and interest. In this event the most useful role for the teacher is probably to be even more consistent and emphatic in her use of symbols so that letters and words and numbers become a reality within a child's own life situation.

Generally speaking, today's pre-school children bring a good deal more variety of ideational subject matter to school than the children of pre-television days. Are they more knowledgeable and sophisticated, or more confused in thought and feeling; more excited and alert or more passive and dependent on outside stimulation? Undoubtedly the effects of television vary from child to child, depending on other influences in their lives. The important thing is that nursery school competes successfully, is very real and very satisfying; a place for self effort and self realization, not a pastime; also a place which has some predictability and sufficient calm to allow the child to consolidate experiences. For the teacher this means a ready pick up of a child's new preoccupation with ingenuity in turning this into constructive interest and activity at a child like level. The topic may be anything from flying saucers to deep-sea diving to heart transplants. Also, it becomes important for adults to keep in mind that young children can worry, especially about human events which they witness on television but cannot grasp or easily put into words. Birth, death, fighting, cruelty, sickness—any number of things may require airing by a teacher in simple, meaningful fashion. These days teachers, like parents, must hold themselves in readiness to deal with the unexpected notions put forward by young children. In short, teachers need to be alert not only to how the child thinks but to what he is trying to think about.

Teaching for social development. At present investigators in early childhood education are giving relatively little attention to the social aspects of the young child's development. In fact, sociability in the nursery school sometimes is considered to be a deterrent to cognitive learning. However, teachers know well that interaction among the children is a perpetual feature of nursery school life. It cannot be deleted and therefore plans are necessary. The question is what goals should be envisaged for current nursery school programming. While child study has not provided exact guidelines for social learning, findings from research and clinical investigation have shown the psychological importance of peer relations in the child's total development. Sociometric studies carried out in nursery school indicate that young children already are in the process of forming and sustaining personal relations with one another. This means that deeper psychological processes are at work than previously believed. Sibling studies reveal the impact which one child has on another. Studies of older children and adolescents indicate that the outcome of learning and development in this area is critical for the individual's final maturity. In the long run the individual lives not with his adults but among his peers.

From the child's point of view, a child who attends a nursery school or day nursery is captive in a social group so that he must adapt in some way. Before he can acquire the abilities for compatible interaction, he must gain a sense of identity among equals. He must feel his way toward accepting other children when his own sense of adequacy is still uncertain and also gain assurance that he is accepted. The alternative to these positive acquisitions is that the child learns to fear his contemporaries or to be frustrated with them as intruders. The pattern of relationship which young children gradually can achieve may be termed inter-independence, that is, to become willing to support each other's efforts. Interdependence will come later.

In the past when social learning first became a goal in pre-school education, a laissez-faire teaching approach was frequently adopted which allowed the children to learn by free social interaction in a protective environment. This method encouraged a high degree of social involvement so that a child's interest in social activity could outweigh his interest and effort in other areas of learning. Undoubtedly free social play is still necessary to allow for initiative and experimentation in the art of social living and in the discovery of mutual relations. But new knowledge of the processes of development suggests that young children need the same kind of teaching help for social learning as for other learning tasks. It is evident that within the nursery school their activity programme must be kept in balance. The emphasis in free-choice play periods can be varied. It can be social or content oriented depending on the teacher's plan, the arrangements of the set up and her expectations, guidance and controls. The same is true in planning group sessions. Without ruling out social interchange the children's attention can be directed primarily toward the subject matter under consideration. Irrespective of content these adult structured situations give the teacher a good opportunity for direct social instruction.

Of course, verbal exchange among children has an important bearing on cognitive as well as social learning. During free play the children often indulge in experimental and playful use of language especially when their relationship is compatible. This has been shown in sociometric research. This kind of learning, although seemingly childish, has a place in the nursery school programme as has learning to communicate with each other about more serious matters. Helping the children to work together as part of a cognitive project will encourage what might be called intellectual co-operation and therefore gives the project a dual value. Since in the long run a child will be called on to use his intelligence in a social world, this combination of cognitive and social learning has merit.

The incidental method of teaching can be used not only to help the children in solving social problems but also to talk to them about social things. The teacher can draw their attention to each other and themselves and to their feelings. She can encourage social effort and point out social achievements as well as failures. Children need words with which to think socially. Percepts and concepts as well as skills are part of social learning and the same principles of stage by stage cognitive development apply. The trouble is that children are inconsistent in their interaction with each other so that percepts are confusing for a young child and concepts are not easily established. The teacher's help is needed to clarify the children's social understanding. Both structured and unstructured learning situations of a social nature can be arranged and teaching can be individual or in groups. Cognitive-social play materials including pictures, dolls, puppets and family and school models as well as dramatic play are useful for teaching.

Children who grow up in culturally deprived homes may have little teaching at home in social percepts and concepts so that the teacher's contribution will be of particular value. Again, day nurseries have a special role to play in guiding the child's social learning and development since most of his play with contemporaries is at the nursery. However, living in a group all day may be overwhelming for a young child. Relief can be arranged by alternating social, less social and non-social activities and by ensuring that the child has time and place for quiet. Some children will need a good deal more help than others to manage socially. A confident relationship with adults appears to be necessary to relieve the anxieties aroused by other children. This means that a child who is withdrawing or in conflict with his peers will need more attention given to relations with adults. The teacher's support will help him to attain the self assurance which is necessary for successful interaction with his equals.

The development of social relations, whether with adults or contemporaries, is a cognitive process as well as a matter of affective development. So, as teachers and children are living and working and talking together, the children are gaining experience in becoming social beings; in doing so they are making real use of their intellect. After all the child is a whole person and his development, although multi-dimensional, is of one piece and it proceeds in orderly fashion. Therefore in an integrated programme the teacher will have all her teaching goals for a child in mind emphasizing each to suit his developmental readiness. Often she will be teaching for several purposes at once. Her all-encompassing goal will be that a child progresses fully in the direction of maturity.

Bibliography

1. Academic and Scientific

Ainsworth, M.D., Andry, R.G., Harlow, R.G., Lebovici, S., Mead, M., Prugh, D.G., Wootton, B. *Deprivation of Maternal Care. A Reassessment of its Effects.* Public Health Papers, No. 14. Geneva: World Health Organization, 1962.

Ainsworth, M.D.S. *Object Relations, Dependency, and Attachment: a theoretical review of the infant-mother relationship.* (USPHS grant R01 HD 01712) *Child Development,* 1969, 40, 969-1025.

Allport, G.W. *Becoming. Basic Considerations for a Psychology of Personality.* New Haven: Yale University Press, 1955.

Almy, M., Chittenden, E. & Miller, P. *Young Children's Thinking. Studies of some aspects of Piaget's theory.* New York: Teachers College Press, Teachers College, Columbia University, 1966.

Blatz, W.E. *The Five Sisters, a study of child psychology.* Toronto: McClelland and Stewart, 1938.

—— *Human Security. Some Reflections.* Toronto: University of Toronto Press, 1966.

—— *Understanding the Young Child.* Toronto: McClelland and Stewart, 1944.

Bott, H.M. *Personality Development in Young Children.* Child Development Series, No. 2. Toronto: University of Toronto Press, 1934.

Bowlby, J. *Attachment and Loss.* Vol. II. *Separation; Anxiety and Anger.* London: Hogarth, 1973.

—— *Maternal Care and Mental Health.* Monograph Series, No. 2. Geneva: World Health Organization, 1952.

Brearley, M. (ed.) *The Teaching of Young Children. Some Applications of Piaget's Learning Theory.* New York: Schocken Books, 1970.

93

Brockman, L., Whiteley, J., & Zubek, J. *Child Development: Selected Readings*. Toronto: McClelland and Stewart, 1973. (See particularly chapters 3, 15, 26 and 36.)

Davis, C. *Room to Grow. A Study of Parent-Child Relationships*. Toronto: University of Toronto Press, 1966.

Erikson, E.H. Identity and the Life Cycle: Selected Papers. *Psychological Issues*. Vol. I, No. 1, Monograph 1, 1959. New York: International Universities Press.

Flint, B.M. *The Child and the Institution. A Study of Deprivation and Recovery*. Toronto: University of Toronto Press, 1966.

—— *The Security of Infants*. Toronto: University of Toronto Press, 1959.

Frost, J.L. (ed.) *Revisiting early childhood education*. New York: Holt, Rinehart and Winston, 1973.

Gesell, A. & Ilg, F.L. *Infant and Child in the Culture of Today*. New York: Harper, 1943.

Johnson, H.M. *Children in the Nursery School*. New York: John Day, 1928. (republished, New York: Agathon Press, 1972, with an introductory essay by Barbara Biber.)

Meeker, M.N. *The Structure of Intellect. Its Interpretation and Uses*. Columbus, Ohio: Charles E. Merrill, 1969.

Meyers, C.E., & Dingman, H.F. Factor Analytic and Structure of Intellect Models in the Study of Mental Retardation. Monograph Supplement to *American Journal of Mental Deficiency*, Vol. 70, No. 4, January, 1966, 7-25.

Northway, M.L., & Weld, L. *Sociometric Testing: a Guide for Teachers*. Toronto: University of Toronto Press, 1957.

Piaget, J. *Six Psychological Studies*. New York: Random House, 1967.

Spodek, B. (ed.) *Early Childhood Education*. Englewood Cliffs, N.J.: Prentice Hall, 1973.

Stott, L.H., & Ball, R.S. Infant and pre-school mental tests: Review and Evaluation. *Monographs of the Society for Research in Child Development*, Serial No. 101, 1965, Vol. 30, No. 3.

White, B.L., & Watts, J.C. *Experience and Environment. Major Influences on the Development of the Young Child*. Vol. 1. Englewood Cliffs, N.J.: Prentice-Hall, 1973.

2. Practices in the Nursery School

Canadian Council of Social Development. *Day Care: National Guidelines for the development of day care services for children.* 55 Parkdale Ave., Box 3505, Station C, Ottawa, Ont. K1Y 4G1.

Caplan, F., & Caplan, T. *The Power of Play.* New York: Doubleday, 1973.

Fletcher, M., & Denison, M. *The New Highroad of Song for Nursery Schools and Kindergartens.* Toronto: Gage, 1960.

—— *A Nursery Revue, Songs and Playlets.* Boston: Boston Music Co., 1955.

Fowke, E. *Sally Go Round the Sun. 300 Songs, Rhymes and Games of Canadian Children.* Toronto: McClelland and Stewart, 1969.

Ginott, H. *Between Teacher and Child.* New York: Macmillan, 1972.

Green, M., & Woods, E. *A Nursery School Handbook for Teachers and Parents.* Sierra Madre Community Nursery School Association, Sierra Madre, California 91024, 1963.

Jones, M.M. *Guiding Your Child from Two to Five.* New York: Harcourt Brace and World, 1967.

Landreth, C. *Preschool Learning and Teaching.* New York: Harper & Row, 1972.

Mallum, M.A. *Santa Monica City Schools Curriculum Guide.* California Children's Centers, Directors and Supervisors Association, 4568 West 135th Hawthorne, California 90250, 1970.

Panabaker, L. *Lucille Panabaker's Song Book.* Toronto: Peter Martin Associates, 1968.

Pitcher, E., & Ames, L. *The Guidance Nursery School.* New York: Harper and Row, 1964.

Read, K. *The Nursery School: A Human Relations Laboratory.* (5th ed.) Philadelphia: W.B. Saunders, 1971.

Rudolph, M. *From Hand to Head. A handbook for teachers of Preschool Programs.* New York: McGraw-Hill, Webster Division, 1972.

Seeger, R.C. *American Folk Songs for Children in Home, School and Nursery School.* Garden City, N.Y.: Doubleday, 1948.

Spodek, B. *Teaching in the Early Years.* Englewood Cliffs, N.J.: Prentice-Hall, 1972.

Stant, M. *The Young Child. His activities and materials.* Englewood Cliffs, N.J.: Prentice-Hall, 1972.
Stone, L., & Church, J. *Childhood and Adolescence.* (3rd. ed.) New York: Random House, 1973.